Food studies for caterers

David R. Watson

CAMBRIDGE
UNIVERSITY PRESS

Published by the Press Syndicate of the University of Cambridge
The Pitt Building, Trumpington Street, Cambridge CB2 1RP
40 West 20th Street, New York, NY 10011-4211, USA
10 Stamford Road, Oakleigh, Victoria 3166, Australia

First published 1992

Printed in Great Britain by Scotprint Ltd, Musselburgh, Scotland

A catalogue record for this book is available from the British Library

ISBN 0 521 40936 5 paperback

Text illustrations by Julian Page

Acknowledgements
Table 2.1 is reproduced by kind permission of the International Association
of Milk, Food and Environmental Sanitarians Inc., Ames, Iowa, USA; Table
11.1 by permission of Edward Arnold.

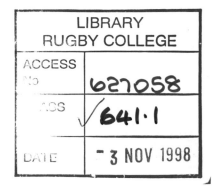

Contents

LIBRARY
RUGBY COLLEGE

Contents

Preface

This book is aimed at all personnel working in the catering industry or teaching catering. It will be especially useful to full- and part-time catering students studying the City and Guilds 706 syllabus, Cooking for the Catering Industry, and the BTEC national and diploma courses in catering.

The hygiene section is aimed to equip students with sufficient understanding to sit the Institution of Environmental Health Officers (IEHO) or Royal Institute for Public Health and Hygiene (RIPHH) exams in food hygiene.

Students studying catering have, in my experience, little scientific background and lack the confidence to develop a scientific understanding, despite its relevance to the catering industry. Caterers are also under great pressure to increase their awareness of hygiene and healthy eating. In view of this I have tried to make the text neither so simplistic or superficial as to be of little value, nor so advanced as to be off-putting to the general caterer. I have kept detail to a minimum and tried to make the text relevant to the student of general catering.

At the end of each chapter there is a section on 'Things to do' which develops in a practical way concepts taught in the text. Some practicals require specialised laboratory facilities, but others can be done in the kitchen. There are also questions about the text which will allow students to assess their understanding of the material covered.

I hope the text will be of value as a teaching aid to lecturers and also to non-student caterers wishing to develop their understanding of catering science and hygiene.

David R. Watson

The law and the caterer

Catering staff who are involved in the preparation and serving of food for sale to the public are obliged by the law to abide by certain rules and regulations. The laws are passed to provide guidelines for the *minimum* standards of hygiene that a customer may confidently expect when dining at a restaurant, café or other catering establishment.

The two most important regulations concerning the general caterer are: the **Food Act 1984** and the **Food Hygiene Regulations 1970**.

The Food Act 1984

This is a lengthy and involved Act of Parliament, most of which can be ignored by the general caterer. However, two sections are very important. Section 1 states that it is illegal either to do anything to food that makes it harmful to health or to offer for sale any food which has been made harmful to health. Section 2 says that it is an offence to offer for sale any food which is not of the nature, substance or quality demanded by the purchaser.

In other words, if customers ask for Cheddar cheese and are given Edam, or ask for halibut and are given cod, clearly they are not getting foods of the **nature** demanded.

If the food sold to a customer contains some ingredient that the customer is not made aware of, for example a preservative in cooked meat, then he/she is not being given food of the **substance** asked for because that ingredient, as far as the customer is concerned, should not be there.

Finally, food must not be spoiled in any way that would affect its **quality**, for example day-old bread must not be sold as freshly baked that day.

Inferior food *can* be sold so long as it is made quite clear to the customer why the food is inferior, for example damaged cans or packets past their sell-by-date must be clearly labelled as such. However, Section 8 states that it is an offence to offer for sale food which is unfit for human consumption.

The Food Hygiene Regulations 1970 and the Food Hygiene [Amendment] Regulations 1990

These regulations apply to any premises running a food business and affect not only the managers and owners of such premises, but anyone who handles food or cleans equipment that comes into contact with food.

Anyone failing to observe these regulations whose duty it is to do so can be prosecuted, for example managers who fail to ensure that their staff follow the Food Hygiene Regulations, or food handlers or cleaners of equipment who do not observe hygienic practices when carrying out their tasks. In addition, those working on food-handling premises can be prosecuted if they are found to have helped violate the Food Hygiene Regulations.

All foods are covered by the regulations if they are intended for human consumption, with the exception of milk – it has its own regulations – and water. The penalties for breaking the Food Hygiene Regulations are a fine of £2000 and/or imprisonment for up to two years.

Personal hygiene

All parts of a food handler's body likely to come into contact with food must be kept as clean as possible. This means not only the hands and forearms, but any other part of the body that the hands are likely to come into contact with, such as the neck and hair.

Food handlers must wear clean and washable overclothing and must not spit or smoke when handling food or when in a room where food is being handled. Any cuts must be covered with a suitable dressing and any illness must be reported to a supervisor. If suffering from typhoid, paratyphoid, dysentery or food-poisoning, a food handler must notify the local medical health officer.

Handling of food

Food must be protected from the risk of contamination: raw and cooked foods must be kept separate, and food must not come into contact with dirty surfaces, waste material and food unfit for human consumption.

Food must be kept at least 18 inches above the ground, and unwrapped food must be kept covered or screened from contamination from sneezes, insects and the like. Materials used for wrapping food must be clean, and printed material like newspapers may only be used for raw vegetables or uncooked game.

Foods such as meat, fish, imitation cream, eggs, milk or any foods containing these substances must be cooled below 8 °C or heated above 63 °C as soon as possible after they come onto the premises. Similarly once such foods have been cooked, they have to be kept at these temperatures until served.

Animals must not be allowed to come into contact with any food, and animal feed must not be kept in any food room.

The food premises

Personal washing and sanitary facilities

All food premises should have an adequate provision of clean hand-basins supplying hot and cold water for all staff engaged in the handling of food. An adequate supply of soap, nail brushes and drying facilities must also be provided.

Toilets should be clean, well lit and well ventilated, and in working order. They should be so positioned that no offensive odours can penetrate any food room and must not be used as a food room or for storing food, utensils or cleaning materials. A NOW WASH YOUR HANDS notice must be placed so that users of the toilets can easily see it.

Food rooms

Food rooms should be adequately lit and ventilated and must not be used for sleeping or open directly into a room used for sleeping.

The food room should be built from materials that can be effectively cleaned. This will help to discourage infestation by pests. No refuse or waste should be allowed to remain in any food room; any such waste must be stored at a suitable site well away from the food room.

Provision of other facilities

First aid material must be readily available to food handlers, and space must be provided to accommodate outdoor clothing.

Administration of the law

It is the task of environmental health officers and the police to make sure that the laws relating to food are enforced. An environmental health officer is employed by every local authority, and one of his/her main responsibilities is to inspect the standard of food hygiene in food premises such as shops, restaurants and hotels. He/she has the power to enter premises, using force if necessary, and can seize food or take samples of food, which may be sent for analysis.

The environmental health officer may give warning of inspection, but usually doesn't. Within one week of the inspection he/she can send the owner of the inspected premises an improvement notice, listing all the faults and how they are to be put right – usually within a period of one month. He/she may then inspect the premises again to see if the improvements have been made. If, however, the environmental health officer considers that the continued use of the premises would be dangerous to health, he/she can apply to the court for a closure order which will not be lifted until the improvements listed by the officer have been carried out.

If the owner is convicted under the Food Act 1984 or the Food Hygiene

Regulations, he/she may be prevented – by a closure order – from carrying on a food business from those premises for up to two years, but he/she may appeal after six months. If there is a danger to public health, for example following an outbreak of food-poisoning traced to a particular establishment, an emergency closure can be carried out, giving the owner only three days' notice. A copy of the Order must be fixed to the premises where it can be clearly seen.

Food Hygiene [Amendment] Regulations 1990

The objective of these regulations, some of which came into effect on 1 April 1991, is to reduce the risks of contamination of food by such food-poisoning bacteria as *Listeria monocytogenes* and *Salmonella* (see Chapter 8). The regulations are being introduced over a period of time to allow businesses to buy new equipment to meet the lower temperature requirements, but it is hoped that the changeover will be completed straight away. The regulations apply to the temperature of the food and not the air temperature, which will usually be below that of the food. From 1 April 1991 all foods covered by the regulations must be kept at or below 8°C (previously 10°C). These include:

soft cheeses
patés
all ready-prepared meals, cooked meats and other prepared foods which are
    to be eaten without further cooking
smoked or cured fish or meat
desserts which have a pH above 4.5
prepared vegetable salads including those containing fruits
sandwiches, filled rolls and similar bread products containing meat, fish,
    eggs and vegetables
cream cakes.

From 1 April 1993 the following foods are to be stored at or below 5°C:

soft cheeses, including those which have been cut or otherwise removed
    from the whole cheese
cooked products which have been prepared for consumption without the
    necessity for further cooking or reheating, e.g. Scotch eggs, cooked
    poultry, pork pies, sandwich fillings
smoked or cured fish or meats
sandwiches or filled rolls, unless they are intended to be sold within 24
    hours from the time of preparation.

Foods exempt from temperature control include foods which have been processed in a way which prevents the growth of pathogenic micro-organisms, e.g. dehydrated foods, canned and bottled foods, bread, biscuits, hard cheese, dry pasta, dry mixes for coffee, and so on.

Food which is eaten hot, that is over 63°C, may be kept for up to two hours before being sold. Food which is to be eaten cold within four hours of its preparation may be kept at room temperature for that time. Food may also be displayed at room temperature for up to four hours – sweet trolleys and cheese boards, for example – but no more food than is reasonably necessary for the purpose should be displayed at one time.

Delivery vehicles

From 1 April 1991 large delivery vehicles must maintain a temperature of 8°C or lower, when delivering foods covered by the regulations.

From 1 April 1992 *all* delivery vehicles, large and small, must maintain a temperature of 8°C or lower, when delivering foods covered by the regulations.

From 1 April 1993 large delivery vehicles must deliver all foods covered by the regulations at or below the temperature at which they are stored – either 5°C or 8°C. Small delivery vehicles (less than 7.5 tons gross weight) will not be obliged in 1993 to carry any foods at 5°C; they may continue to deliver foods at 8°C.

Test yourself

1 Members of the public preparing their family meal in their kitchen at home are exempt from the hygiene laws. True or false.

2 Under the Food Act 1984 which of the following is *not* an offence?
   a selling venison as beef
   b selling slimy, off-smelling meat
   c selling day-old bread labelled as stale
   d selling dog meat for human consumption

3 Which of the following catering staff is *not* covered by the Food Hygiene Regulations 1970?
   a restaurant owner
   b hotel manager
   c cleaner of kitchen surfaces
   d hotel receptionist

4 Which of the following *can* be stored between 8°C and 63°C before serving?
   a eggs
   b milk
   c baked custard tart
   d fish

5 Which of the following illnesses must be reported to the local medical health officer?
   a flu
   b dysentery
   c measles
   d chicken pox

6 What is the minimum height above ground that food must be kept?
  a 20 inches
  b 16 inches
  c 12 inches
  d 18 inches

7 Name three things that must be provided in a washroom for staff engaged in food handling.
  a
  b
  c

8 Say which of the following is true and which false.
  a A NOW WASH YOUR HANDS notice must be clearly displayed in the washroom.
  b Waterproof dressings must be readily available for all kitchen staff.
  c Space must be provided for outdoor clothing.
  d Coffee percolators must be provided for all kitchen staff.

9 Between which temperatures must food *not* be kept whilst waiting to be served?
  a _____   **b** _____

10 Say which of the following is true and which false.
  a An environmental health officer can inspect public food premises at any time.
  b An environmental health officer can use force to gain access if necessary.
  c An environmental health officer has to give notice of an inspection.
  d An environmental health officer can close a business down within three days if the danger is serious enough.

Now check your answers with the text.

Food – *you the food handler*

two

As we have seen in Chapter 1 all people who come into contact with food professionally are obliged by law to observe and maintain strict standards of hygiene.

Catering demands a great deal from those who work in the industry: they have to work long, unsocial hours in hot and sometimes cramped conditions and have to satisfy customers by getting their orders to them at exactly the right time. As a result, standards are not always maintained as they should be, and the clientele, the dining public, may suffer.

For a caterer the worst situation that can occur is for a customer to become ill with food-poisoning after eating at his or her premises.

Food-poisoning

Is the number of cases increasing?

Food-poisoning is a notifiable disease and all cases should be reported to the Medical Officer for Environmental Health. It is part of the officer's job to record the number of cases which occur in his/her health district. However, as the symptoms for food-poisoning can be quite mild and may be described merely as 'an upset tummy' or put down to over-eating, many cases go unreported. In fact, the number of cases reported represents only a small proportion of food-poisoning incidences, but as the graph in Figure 2.1 shows, the number is increasing.

This increase is due to a variety of reasons. The public are more aware of hygiene standards and the possibility of food-poisoning, and so are more likely to seek medical advice for an upset stomach. Thus more cases are reported than in the past.

As eating out has become more popular, many people who know little about the problems associated with the bulk handling of foods are setting up restaurants and cafés or serving bar meals in their pubs. As no professional qualification is needed to set up a catering business, many prospective caterers are ignorant of their legal obligations to maintain standards of hygiene.

The causes

Food-poisoning is caused by certain types of bacteria (*Salmonella*, for

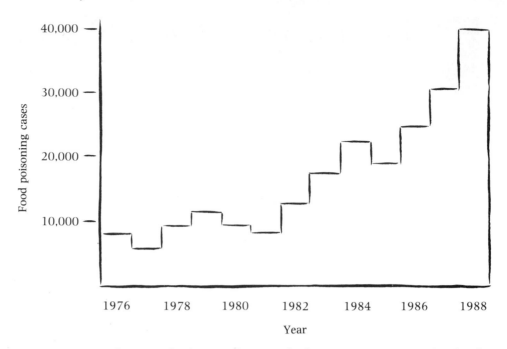

Figure 2.1   Notification of infectious diseases: food poisoning 1976–88 (England and Wales). From *Communicable Diseases Report*, PHLS Communicable Disease Surveillance Centre, London, 1991.

example) which enter the body, usually in contaminated food, and either cause an infection or produce toxic chemicals (toxins) which cause symptoms such as vomiting, stomach cramps and diarrhoea.

Foods must be handled properly and kept at the correct temperature to prevent bacteria from growing in them. Usually it is failure to do so that causes food-poisoning.

Recent studies in Britain and the United States have analysed the backgrounds to large numbers of food-poisoning outbreaks to determine the causes. The findings are shown in Table 2.1. The commonest cause was found to be preparing the food too early and keeping it at a temperature below 63°C (room temperature) before serving, instead of cooling and refrigerating it. In addition, inadequate reheating, insufficient thawing, and cross-contamination were important factors contributing to food-poisoning.

The stages leading up to an outbreak

An outbreak of food-poisoning can be separated into three stages which make up the food-poisoning chain:

CONTAMINATION ⟶ MULTIPLICATION ⟶ CONSUMPTION

Table 2.1   **Factors contributing to foodborne disease (%)**

Factor	Roberts (1982) England & Wales 1970–79 1044 outbreaks	Bryan (1986) USA 1977–82 766 outbreaks
Preparation too far in advance (> 12 hours)	61	25
Holding at ambient/room temperature	40	21
Inadequate cooling/refrigeration	32	20
Inadequate reheating	29	9
Undercooking/underprocessing	15	14
Improper warmholding	6	9
Cross-contamination	6	4
Inadequate thawing	6	1

Sources: Roberts, D. 'Factors contributing to the outbreaks of food poisoning in England and Wales 1970–1979', *Journal of Hygiene* (Cambridge), 89, pp. 491–8; Bryan, F. 'Risks of practices, procedures and processes that lead to outbreaks of foodborne diseases', *Journal of Food Protection*, 51 (1986), pp. 663–73.

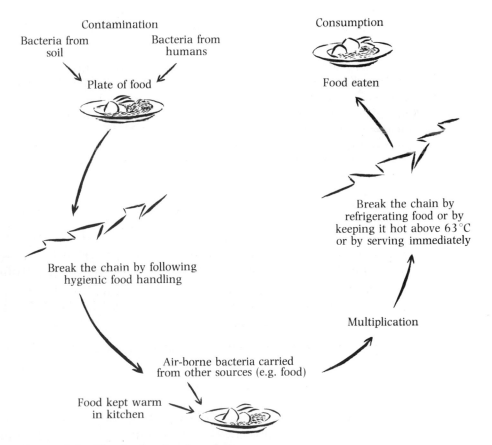

Figure 2.2   The food-poisoning chain

Contamination is bacteria on or in food. Food-poisoning bacteria are present on raw meat and fish, in the soil surrounding vegetables and in large numbers on certain parts of the human body (see section on Personal hygiene in this chapter). When food handlers touch contaminated food or parts of the body such as hair, face or neck, they must wash their hands thoroughly to prevent the spread of bacteria to clean food.

Multiplication is the increase in the number of bacteria on food. A single bacterium is unlikely to cause food-poisoning, and the number of bacteria must build up to an infective dose or produce large quantities of toxin before they can cause illness. Because they are warm, kitchens provide the ideal climate for the maximum rate of growth of bacteria and harmful numbers are reached on contaminated food within hours.

Consumption means eating food, and, if it is contaminated, consuming bacteria as well. Unfortunately it is not always apparent that a food has become dangerous. Bad odours, if they have been produced at all, may be masked by the flavouring in the food. The only way of guessing if a food is dangerous is by assessing its chances of contamination and how long it has spent in the warmth of the kitchen before being served.

Breaking the food-poisoning chain

To prevent food-poisoning the chain must be broken and this can be done in two ways: **prevention of contamination** by following hygienic food-handling practices (see section on Personal hygiene below) and **prevention of multiplication** by either keeping food at the correct temperature (putting it in the fridge or keeping it hot above 63 °C) if it is not needed immediately or serving the food straight away and not giving the bacteria time to grow.

Personal hygiene

The human skin and gut are prime sources of bacteria, and the fingers are the main agents for the transfer of bacteria onto food. The most important thing to remember when working with food is that your fingers are *never* clean. Keep the handling of foods to a minimum, especially perishable food such as cooked meats.

When to wash your hands

Wash your hands as frequently as possible but especially at the following times:

- on entering the kitchen
- after a break, especially if you have been smoking
- after going to the toilet – bacteria can get through many thicknesses of toilet paper and are also present on the flushing lever and on handles of doors and taps

- after touching your face (for example, rubbing your eyes, picking or blowing your nose, scratching your ear, combing your hair, licking your fingers)
- after touching raw food
- before handling perishable foods
- between jobs
- after disposing of refuse
- after handling cleaning materials
- after eating

Looking after your hands

- Keep nails short, clean and free from varnish.
- Cover any cuts with a waterproof, coloured dressing so it can be easily seen should it come off in the food being prepared.
- Do not wear jewellery.

Hand washing

Hands must always be washed in a basin specially reserved for such a purpose and no other. Hot water, soap and a nail brush should be used to wash away bacteria. Hands should be dried under a hot-air dryer or with paper towels or a continuous roller towel.

Dirty habits

Because saliva contains a large number of bacteria, the following habits can spread food-poisoning bacteria:

- **spitting** – illegal in food preparation areas
- **coughing and sneezing** – both spray food with bacteria from saliva
- **tasting** – use a spoon, which should be washed afterwards; *never* use your finger
- **smoking** – illegal in food preparation areas; touching the lips to remove the cigarette brings your fingers into contact with saliva

In addition to these possible sources of contamination, there is another:

- **chef's cloth** – used for a multitude of purposes and very quickly becomes heavily contaminated with bacteria. Use it only as an insulator when handling hot utensils and never for wiping hands or food: it may look as if it's clean, but it never is.

Protective clothing

The Food Hygiene Regulations 1970 require anyone working with food to wear sufficient clean and washable clothing.

An apron does not provide sufficient cover. More extensive protective clothing should be worn, and it must be washable and kept clean. No outdoor clothing should be worn in a food preparation area and, similarly, protective clothing should not be worn outside.

The hair on our heads is continually falling out and is contaminated by bacteria, so a hat must be worn to prevent hairs from dropping into food. The hat should hold *all* the hair. Unfortunately the traditional male chef's hat does not do this and is purely cosmetic. Tradition is hard to change, so while chef's hats continue to be decorative rather than functional, a chef's hair should be kept as short as possible.

Figure 2.3   Sources of bacteria

Cross-contamination

This is the transfer of bacteria from one item to another. It may occur directly, for example between raw and cooked meat placed on top of each other, or by indirect cross-contamination, where fingers, a kitchen utensil or even a fly pick up bacteria from a source and transfer it onto food.

Certain items in the kitchen area are dangerous sources of food-poisoning bacteria: raw meat, soil on vegetables, the toilet. Such items need to be handled with caution to prevent transfer of bacteria onto foods such as cooked meat, fish, soups or sauces, all of which provide ideal conditions for the bacteria to multiply.

To prevent cross-contamination:

- Never let raw food or its juices come into contact with cooked food.
- Never place raw and cooked food on the same dish.
- Always store cooked food above raw foods in the fridge.
- Always wash your hands after handling raw food and before handling cooked food.
- Always wash knives and other implements used on raw food before using them on cooked food.
- Use separate chopping boards for raw and cooked foods. (Colour coding may help here, either by labelling boards with coloured tape or by using different coloured chopping boards.)

Things to do

1 Contact your Medical Officer for Environmental Health for information on the number of food-poisonings in your area.

2 Observe colleagues working in your kitchen. Are they following hygienic food-handling practices?

3 Check the steps taken in your kitchen to avoid cross-contamination. Tick the boxes in the following checklist if the correct procedure is followed in your kitchen.
  a Raw food is separated from cooked food by:
     preparing raw and cooked foods in separate areas of the kitchen
     placing raw and cooked foods on separate dishes
     storing raw food below cooked food in the fridge
  b Hands are always washed after:
     going to the toilet
     a break
     smoking
     touching face or hair
     handling raw food and before handling cooked food
     eating
     emptying waste bins

c Knives and other implements are washed after use on raw food and before use on cooked food.

d Are separate chopping boards used for preparing raw food and cooked food?

4 We can investigate whether different surfaces have bacteria on them or not by performing simple experiments using Petri dishes, agar-agar (a vegetarian substitute for gelatine) and sterile swabs. If you have the equipment, try the following three experiments, which should be attempted only under supervision. Before you begin, read carefully the following points, which should be always be borne in mind when handling micro-organisms.

Notes on handling micro-organisms

- **After introducing bacteria onto the agar in the Petri dish, seal with a cross of Sellotape to hold the two halves together.**

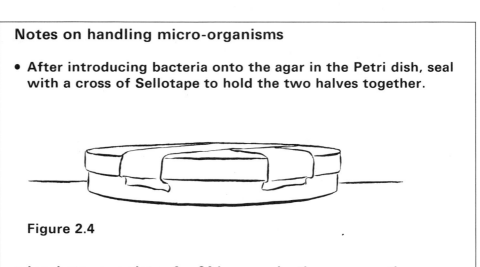

Figure 2.4

- **Incubate your plates for 24 hours only; then remove them from the incubator and store them in a fridge or cool place until ready for viewing.**
- ***Never* remove the lid from an incubated Petri dish; always make your observations through the top or from the underside.**
- **Dispose of your Petri dishes immediately after viewing, but first place them in an autoclave for 20 minutes.**
- **Always wash your hands after handling Petri dishes, and never eat or drink in the laboratory.**

First of all, prepare four Petri dishes by placing enough nutrient agar in them to cover the bottom.

a Take the lid off a Petri dish for ten minutes and then replace it.

b Quickly lift the lid of a second dish and place your fingertips gently onto the agar surface or lay a hair onto the surface of the agar and replace the lid immediately.

c Use a sterile swab to take samples from food preparation surfaces, items of equipment, crockery or other areas of the kitchen, and transfer the bacteria to the agar plate. (If you wish to keep the sources separate, you will need to prepare more Petri dishes.)

After sampling, seal the lids using Sellotape and incubate the Petri dishes for 24 hours at 37°C. This will allow the individual bacteria present on your sampling surfaces to grow and form visible colonies.

We can measure the extent of contamination by counting the number of colonies that have sprouted. The larger colonies will represent heavily contaminated areas, which would pose a health hazard. Small areas of bacteria would indicate a cleaner environment.

Test yourself

1 Which of the following is *not* a possible reason for the increase in food-poisoning outbreaks?
  a customers becoming more aware of hygiene
  b untrained staff
  c increased pressure on staff so they cut corners
  d people eating too much

2 Food-poisoning is caused by poor standards of hygiene allowing bacteria to contaminate food. True or false?

3 Arrange the following sentences in the order of the food-poisoning chain.
  a Food-poisoning occurs.
  b Bacteria are transferred onto food.
  c The food is eaten.
  d Poor storage allows the bacteria to multiply.
  e Bacteria are present in soil and on raw meat and fish.

4 Between which two temperatures is it dangerous to store food if multiplication of bacteria is to be avoided?

5 Bacteria are always present on your hands. True or false?

6 On which of the following occasions should you wash your hands?
  a on entering the kitchen
  b after a break
  c after rubbing your eyes
  d between jobs
  e after going to the toilet
  f after eating
  g after handling raw vegetables
  h before touching raw meat

7 What three items do you need to wash your hands?

8 Which of the following is illegal in a food preparation area?
  a chef's cloth
  b coughing or sneezing
  c tasting
  d smoking

9 Read the following and pick out the bad hygiene practices which can result in contamination of food.

LUNCHTIME AT LA BELLA SALMON RESTAURANT

Following his break when he had enjoyed his first cigarette of the day, Harry Halitosis went straight back to washing the lettuce he had left to soak in the sink in the kitchen.

Jerry Jerm arrived late, as he had been up most of the night with an upset stomach and was feeling a bit under the weather. He was in a bit of a hurry to get food prepared for the coming lunch, so he removed the frozen chickens from the freezer and placed them in the sink, covering them with hot water before going to change into his whites in the toilets.

Harry, meanwhile, was drying the lettuce using his chef's cloth. He placed it on plates from which he'd wiped away hairs left by the cleaner, who had refused to cover her new hair-do with a hat.

The head chef completed the sauce to go with the chicken and dipped his finger in the pot to sample it.

Jerry removed the chickens from the water – he didn't have time to leave them there for long – trimmed them with his knife, and placed them in the oven to cook. Using the same knife, he began preparing the vegetables, but in his hurry nicked his finger and it began to bleed. He put the finger under cold water to stop the bleeding and then wrapped it with a piece of tissue as there were no plasters in the first aid box, and continued cutting the vegetables.

When he'd finished cleaning the lettuce, Harry began washing up the dirty utensils, throwing them all in together. When they all seemed clean he took them straight out and left them to dry.

Just before the restaurant opened, the two waitresses, Jean and Linda, arrived and immediately started to help garnish the plates with salad. Jean's perfume irritated Linda and she sneezed, covering her mouth with her hand, and then continued with the garnishing. Linda's bracelet and rings were getting in the way so she took them off and placed them in a bowl for safe-keeping.

The head chef examined the finished dishes before they were served and then went to sit down at his desk in a corner of the kitchen to plan the evening menu, confident in the success of the lunch.

Now check your answers with the text.

three

Nutrition and a healthy diet

We, like all living things, are able to move and grow, repair and maintain our bodies and reproduce. During the first twenty years of life we are continually growing; in later years we must maintain the bodies we have built. To enable us to do these things, we need energy and building materials which we get in the form of the food we eat.

The caterer's job is to provide customers with food which is not only appetising but provides the nourishment they need in order to live. The word used to describe our food requirements is **nutrition**, and the items that we need are called **nutrients**.

Nutrients

What are the basic nutrients that we need in our daily diet? They can be put into two groups: those that are needed in large quantities, called **macronutrients**, and those that are needed in much smaller amounts, known as **micronutrients**.

Macronutrients make up most of our diet. They are made up of:

- **carbohydrates** – divided into starches (found in flour and potatoes) and sugars (found in sweet foods and occurring naturally in fruits, honey, vegetables and plants)
- **fats and oils** (together known as **lipids**) – include butter, margarine, lard, suet, sunflower oil, olive oil, corn oil
- **proteins** – found in meat, fish, eggs, milk, dairy produce such as cheese and yoghurt, and pulses such as lentils and beans.

Micronutrients are needed for good health, but in small amounts:

- **vitamins** – found in fruits and vegetables
- **minerals** – include iron (found in meat) and calcium (found in milk)

The two groups contain between them the five main nutrients needed by human beings. In addition we also need water and fibre, which are essential to the proper functioning of our bodies.

Carbohydrates

Over 50 per cent of the Western diet is carbohydrate, and in the Third World the percentage is even higher. We consume so much carbohydrate because it is the body's main source of energy and we need energy to move, to keep the body warm and to enable it to grow. Energy is measured in kilojoules, **kJ**, or kilocalories, **kcal**. ('Kilo' means 1000.) Carbohydrate provides 16 kJ or 3.8 kcal of energy per gram.

The main sources of carbohydrate in our diet are bread, potatoes, carrots, fruit, sugar, cereals (e.g. wheat, oats) and pasta. It is important to note that carbohydrate-rich foods are also the main sources of fibre in our diet. Simple carbohydrates are made by plants using water and air and the energy from sunlight. This process is called **photosynthesis**. The first carbohydrate a plant makes is called **glucose**, which is a sugar found in fruits, honey, sweetcorn and other vegetables. Glucose belongs to a group of carbohydrates called single sugars or **monosaccharides** ('mono' means single, 'saccharide' means sugar). This is the sugar carried in the blood to give us energy. It is used in confectionery, jam-making and brewing. Another monosaccharide used by caterers is **fructose**, which is found in honey and the juices of fruits.

When two single sugars (monosaccharides) are joined together they form a new sugar which is called a **disaccharide** ('di' stands for two). Common table sugar, which is widely used by caterers, is a disaccharide sugar called **sucrose**. It is made by glucose and fructose joining together, and is found in, and extracted from, sugar cane and sugar beet. **Lactose**, the sugar found in milk, and **maltose**, the sugar found in cereals, are also disaccharides. (See Figure 3.1.)

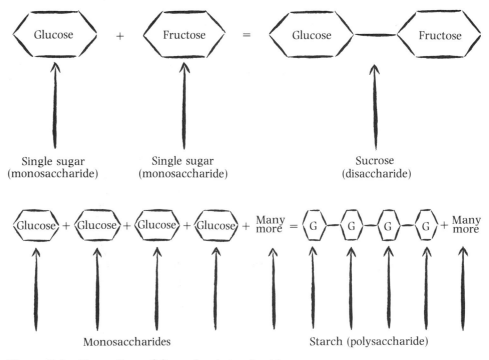

Figure 3.1   Formation of di- and polysaccharides

Both monosaccharides and disaccharides are sweet and dissolve in water to give a sweet solution. However, when single sugars are made into long chains of monosaccharide units called **polysaccharides** ('poly' means many), then they are no longer sweet and do not dissolve in water. Starch is the most widely used polysaccharide in the catering industry and is made up of a chain of 3000 monosaccharides. Starch is found in large quantities in cereals like wheat. It is extracted from the plant and made into flour – wheat flour and corn flour, for example. Another major source of starch is root vegetables such as potatoes.

Fats and oils (lipids)

Fats and oils (the word lipid refers to both) are essential to the body's cell structure. They also form a layer beneath the skin to prevent heat loss, and around our internal organs, for example the heart and the kidneys, to protect against damage.

Lipids are also an important source of energy, containing over twice as much per gram as carbohydrates (37 kJ or 9 kcal per gram). They are not as rich in fibre as carbohydrates, however, especially if they are of animal origin. They are an important source of vitamins, particularly vitamins A, D, E and K. Because fat is slow to digest it prevents hunger sensations longer than other nutrients.

A fat is solid at room temperature, whereas an oil is liquid and runny. Oils can, however, be solidified chemically. This is how products like sunflower oil margarine are made.

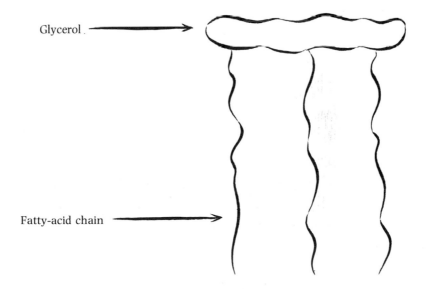

Figure 3.2 Structure of lipids

Fats and oils are made up of two separate sub-units called **glycerol** and **fatty acids**. The fatty acids form a chain attached to a head of glycerol. The fatty-acid chain may be **saturated** or **unsaturated** – it is the saturated lipids which are thought to be associated with heart disease. In general, animal fats contain saturated fatty acids and vegetable oils contain unsaturated fatty acids.

Most foods contain some fat; it may be visible fat like the fat on meat, or invisible fat like that in eggs, mayonnaise and gravy. In general, naturally occurring fat is pure – lard and suet in animals and olive oil, for example. Fats can also exist as a combination or emulsion of fats and water – butter and margarine, for example.

An **emulsion** is formed when two liquids that do not naturally combine (oil and water, for example) are forced together and then chemically stabilised using an **emulsifying agent** or **emulsifier**. Think of a French dressing, which is a mixture of oil and vinegar violently shaken together to make them combine and then stabilised with mustard. Unfortunately the emulsion formed is only temporary and if left to stand the oil will float to the surface of the vinegar. A more permanent emulsion is formed if egg yolk, which contains a naturally occurring emulsifier called **lecithin**, is added. This produces mayonnaise, which, if left to stand, will not separate out.

Many low-fat spreads are emulsions that contain large quantities of water and therefore less energy. Because of their high water content they are unsuitable for frying or baking.

Proteins

Proteins are an essential part of all living cells. A certain amount of protein is present in most foods but it is particularly abundant in milk, meat, eggs and pulses, for example beans and lentils.

Proteins not only form the main structures of our body, we need them for growth, body-building and repairing damaged tissue, too. In addition, proteins can be used to give us a certain amount of energy (17 kJ or 4 kcal per gram) but as this is not their main role, they are not as important in this respect as carbohydrates and fats.

Proteins are made from sub-units called **amino acids**, which are linked together to form a long chain coiled around on itself – like a ball of string – to make a solid structure.

There are 20 different amino acids, which are used to make all the many kinds of protein we need. Our bodies can make most of these amino acids, but there is a small number, called **essential amino acids**, which the body is unable to make. The only way we can obtain these essential amino acids is from the protein foods in our diet. Some protein foods like eggs contain

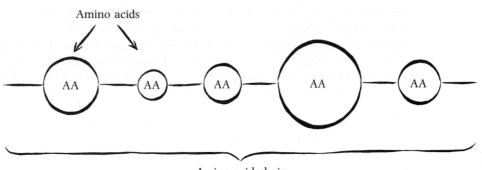

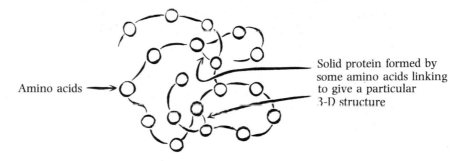

Figure 3.3   Protein structure

Table 3.1   **The biological value of some proteins**

Source of protein	Biological value (marks out of 100)
Mother's milk	100
Eggs	100
Fish	80
Meat	80
Cow's milk	75
Potatoes	70
Liver	65
Rice	55
Soya beans	55
Maize	55
Wheat flour	50
Peas	45
Beans	45

These are not exact figures; they merely give an indication of how complete a source of protein the foods are.
Figures are based on Food and Agriculture Organisation (FAO) and World Health Organisation (WHO) reports.

all the essential amino acids, whereas others like milk, beans and potatoes lack some of them. If the source of protein in a meal lacks any of the essential amino acids, the menu-planner must include a 'complementary' protein food which is rich in those missing amino acids. When meat protein and grain protein are eaten together, the essential amino acids missing in the meat but present in the grain, and vice versa, complement each other.

To make this balancing act somewhat easier, each protein food is given a **biological value**. The higher the value, the more essential amino acids that particular protein food supplies. Eggs have a biological value of 100 as they contain all the essential amino acids, whereas potatoes have a biological value of 70, indicating that some of the essential amino acids are missing. Combinations of foods with high biological values will not necessarily provide all the essential amino acids.

Vitamins

Vitamins needed by the body are split into two categories, those that dissolve in water, like vitamins B and C, and those that dissolve in fats, like vitamins A, D, E and K.

Vitamins are essential for promoting good health; they affect the ageing process and help to prevent disease. They also regulate the building and repair of cells and the release of energy in the body.

Although vitamins are needed only in small amounts, the body has no way of storing some of them so a daily intake is needed. Unfortunately, vitamins are delicate and the amount present in food is affected by its freshness and by the way it's stored, prepared in the kitchen and cooked.

Certain drugs affect vitamin levels in the body. Aspirin and nicotine (acquired by smoking) prevent the body absorbing enough vitamin C; the contraceptive pill affects the levels of certain vitamins and both alcohol and antibiotics stop vitamin B from being absorbed.

Deficiencies in specific vitamins have classic symptoms, for instance vitamin C deficiency is associated with scurvy. An inadequate intake of any vitamin may also cause mild symptoms like tiredness, broken nails, or poor condition of skin, hair or teeth. A person's overall food intake may be high, but vitamin loss can also be high with modern processing methods. It is not uncommon for someone eating a diet of processed foods to show mild deficiency symptoms.

Vitamin losses in food processing and storage
Some vitamins in foods are lost when food is stored in contact with air for as little as one day. Oxygen in the air acts on the food and causes a chemical reaction called **oxidation** which destroys vitamins. Of the vitamin C content of cabbage 30 per cent is lost after one day in storage.

Table 3.2 **Water-soluble vitamins**

Vitamin	What it does	Where it is found	Deficiency symptoms
B_1 (Thiamine)	Helps to get energy from food; needed for healthy heart and nerves	Added to flour and breakfast cereals; brown rice; liver; kidneys; milk; eggs	Loss of appetite; tiredness; irritability; beriberi in extreme cases – muscle wasting, paralysis, death
B_2 (Ribo-flavin)	Contributes to healthy skin; needed for building body tissue, so affects growth rate	Added to cereals; meat; milk; eggs; green vegetables	Poor growth rate; eyes become sensitive to light; sores; cracked lips
Niacin (Nicotinic acid)	Affects growth rate; essential for healthy skin and nerves	Added to flour and cereals; meat; fish; eggs	Loss of appetite; pellagra in extreme cases – dizziness, rough red skin, weakness, death
Folic acid	Essential to the making of blood cells	Liver; kidneys; fish; green leafy vegetables; whole grains; pulses	Tiredness; anaemia
B_6 (Pyridoxine)	Essential to the making of blood cells, healthy blood vessels and nervous system	Liver; kidneys; fish; yeast and yeast products; whole-grain cereals; vegetables	Convulsions in infants – so it is added to baby milks; may cause pre-menstrual tension
B_{12} (Cobalamine)	Essential to healthy blood cells and nervous system	Liver; kidneys; meat in general; eggs; milk; added to breakfast cereals; no B_{12} in vegetables or cereal foods	Anaemia – vegetarians are especially at risk
C (Ascorbic acid)	Essential to the making of new body cells and blood vessels; keeps bones, teeth and gums healthy; may help to fight infections	Citrus fruits (oranges, lemons); potatoes; peppers; tomatoes; cabbage; blackcurrants; strawberries; melons; vitamin C-enriched fruit juices	Spotty skin; slow healing of small cuts and scratches; swelling of gums; weak teeth; scurvy in extreme cases – bleeding gums

Table 3.3 **Fat-soluble vitamins**

Vitamin	What it does	Where it is found	Deficiency symptoms
A	Essential for good vision, especially in dim light; needed for the health of all inner linings of the body	Liver; fish; eggs; milk; added to margarine The body can make its own vitamin A from vegetables like carrots	Dry, sore eyes; conjunctivitis
D	Essential to the development of strong bones and teeth; helps the body to absorb calcium and phosphorus	Added to margarine; cod liver oil; egg yolk; liver Can be made in skin exposed to sunlight	Soft bones in babies; deformed limbs, especially legs – rickets; bone disease in adults
E	Essential for healthy blood cells; essential for reproduction in some animals	Vegetable oils; wheatgerm; oatmeal; lettuce; eggs; liver; meat	Not yet known, but may cause low blood-levels in adults
K	Needed for clotting of blood	Leafy vegetables; eggs; milk	Prolonged bleeding

Thus before the foods even reach the caterers' kitchens, they are likely to suffer vitamin loss. In the process of drying, for example, 50 per cent of vitamin C is lost from dried fruits and vegetables, and 65 per cent of vitamin B is lost from dried meat. (As water is lost, so too are the water-soluble vitamins, though freeze-drying may minimise vitamin loss as it is a faster process.) The canning process, too, results in considerable loss of vitamins, but they are sometimes preserved by the addition of sulphites.

In addition to these hazards, washing and preparing food in the kitchen can allow large quantities of the water-soluble vitamins B and C to be lost.

The nutritional value of frozen food, particularly fruit and vegetables, can be higher than that of the 'fresh' food. The freezing plant is often very close to the growing crop, so once picked, the food can be frozen quickly, thus preserving the nutrient content. However, losses do occur during the preparation of the vegetables for freezing. The blanching process causes 5–10 per cent of vitamin C to be lost.

The longer frozen fruit and vegetables are stored, the greater is the vitamin loss: 50 per cent of vitamin C is lost when food is frozen for over one year.

Vitamin losses during cooking
Vitamins are very susceptible to cooking. The vitamin content of cooked food depends on several factors:

- the method of cooking. The amount of vitamins B and C lost when food is heated varies with the method used. Pressure cooking, microwave cooking and fast, stir-frying methods retain more vitamins than boiling, frying and roasting.
- the amount of contact with oxygen. The greater the area of food exposed to air, the greater the loss of vitamins B and C is – they react with the oxygen in the air. So carrots cut into fine strips a long time before cooking will lose more vitamins through oxidation than those left whole and prepared just before cooking.
- the alkalinity of the cooking liquid. Alkaline solutions like bicarbonate of soda rapidly increase the rate of destruction of vitamins B and C.
- the vitamins' solubility in water. Water used to cook green vegetables absorbs 40 per cent of the vitamin B and 70 per cent of the vitamin C in the food. The more water that is used or the greater the surface area of the food that is exposed to water, the greater is the loss of water-soluble vitamins. Carrot julienne, for example, will lose far more vitamins in cooking than whole carrots. By using the vegetable cooking liquid and fat drippings from meat to make gravy, some of the vitamins can be retained in the final meal. Fewer vitamins are lost when cooking fruit, because the acidity of the fruit helps to stabilise the vitamins.
- the vitamins' solubility in fat. As vitamins A and D are fat-soluble they are lost in the fat drippings from meat.

Vitamin additives
Laws passed after the Second World War to improve poor health required the addition of vitamins to certain basic food items:

- flour – B-group vitamins added
- margarine – vitamins A and D added
- infant milk powders – wide range of vitamins added

Some food product manufacturers voluntarily enrich the nutrient content of their foods to improve the quality of their product:

- breakfast cereals – wide range of vitamins added
- orange juice – vitamin C added
- mashed potatoes – vitamin C added

There is a growing demand for vitamin pills to be taken as a supplement, but it is unnecessary to add anything to a balanced diet containing fresh fruit and vegetables properly prepared. Taking too many of some vitamins, especially vitamin A (as found in liver), can actually poison the body.

Mineral elements

Altogether the body needs 19 different mineral elements, though many are required in tiny amounts. They are essential to the body's functioning and structure, and without them deficiency symptoms occur.

Mineral elements are widely distributed in foods. If care is taken to include

Table 3.4 **Mineral elements**

Mineral	What it does	Where it is found	Deficiency symptoms
Calcium (and phosphorus)	Essential to the development of bones and teeth; especially important in the diet of pregnant women	Milk; bread; cheese; canned fish; beer; hard water	Poor bone formation in children – rickets; bone deformation in adults
Iron	Needed to produce blood cells; especially important in the diet of pregnant and menstruating women	Liver; kidneys; eggs; bread; green vegetables; added to breakfast cereals	Anaemia; lethargy
Sodium	Maintains body fluid levels and healthy nerves	Meat; fish; eggs; milk; manufactured foods like ham, smoked fish; table salt	Heart failure; *excess* causes high blood pressure
Iodine	Essential for the body's hormones	Seafood; sea salt	Swellings in the neck – goitre

on the menu foods containing enough of the main elements, that is calcium, iron and iodine, there will be enough of most of the other mineral elements. Some foods like white flour and breakfast cereals are enriched with minerals.

Water and fibre

Two other items are essential to our diet, but they cannot be classified as nutrients, for although the body will not function properly without them, they are not used in the same way as the other nutrients. They are water and roughage, or fibre.

About 65 per cent of our body is water. Without it the body's chemical reactions, for example making new body tissues, cannot take place. We can survive many days, even weeks, without food, but only a matter of hours without water because we are continually losing it through our urine and sweat. A regular intake is essential.

Fibre is the term given to the part of our diet that we are unable to digest. Another name for it is roughage. Fibre is found only in plant foods (see Chapter 5). It can be divided into two categories depending on whether it will dissolve in water or not:

- soluble fibre – pectin, for example
- insoluble fibre – wheat bran, for example

It has been known for many years that populations who eat plenty of plant materials do not suffer from as much constipation, heart disease, diabetes or cancer of the bowel as people whose diets contain little fibre.

The reasons for this are varied. Foods with insoluble fibre pass through the digestive tract with ease, but those with little or no insoluble fibre pass slowly through the gut (see Chapter 5) and form lumps, resulting in constipation. Some examples of insoluble fibre are brown rice, vegetables and brown bread. Recent research has suggested that soluble fibre may absorb excess cholesterol, and so reduce the risk of developing heart disease. Dietary fibre also adds bulk to the food and therefore satisfies the appetite faster, thus reducing the total amount of food eaten – and helping to prevent over-eating.

A healthy diet

Research has found the incidence of heart disease in Britain to be one of the highest in the world. Two reports, by the National Advisory Committee on Nutrition Education (NACNE) and the Committee of Medical Aspects (COMA) have linked heart disease to our diet, and blamed in particular the amount of fat that we eat.

Heart attacks are caused when the blood vessels supplying the heart with blood become blocked, depriving the heart of oxygen and food so it cannot work to pump blood around the rest of the body. This may happen gradually, causing angina, or suddenly, resulting in an immediate stoppage of the heart – a heart attack. Fat, in particular saturated fats like butter, lard and suet which come from animals, builds up on the inside walls of the blood vessels causing a blockage. Fat is deposited in the arteries from an early age: children of 8–10 years already have fatty bumps in their arteries.

Fat is a concentrated form of energy and we get 20–30 per cent of our energy requirements from fat. NACNE recommends that we get much less of our energy from fat and eat more carbohydrate-rich foods for energy, for example potatoes, pasta and bread.

NACNE also recommends that we should eat less sugar, as excess sugar is converted to fat. This is then stored in the body, thus raising the total amount of fat in the blood.

A lot of the food we eat is highly refined and much of the fibre is removed. It is fibre which forms the roughage part of our diet and maintains a healthy bowel. It is thought fibre consumption reduces the possibility of contracting bowel cancer and even reduces the risk of heart disease.

NACNE recommends, therefore, that we:

- eat less sugar
- eat less fat, especially saturated fat
- eat more fibre

Menu planning

Traditionally, the role of the caterer has been to produce a menu that is enticing and well-balanced in texture, colour, seasonings and sauces. However, more and more clients are becoming nutritionally aware and are scrutinising menus for healthier items.

Providing a variety of choices on an *à la carte* menu leaves the client with the responsibility to choose a nutritious meal. As most Western diets contain a wide variety of foods, our choices will not necessarily ensure we get a nutritionally balanced meal. We may want to have a piece of cake to

Table 3.5 **Dietary reference values for food energy and nutrients for the United Kingdom, 1991: estimated average requirements (EAR) for food energy, protein and iron**

Age	Energy kcals/d (MJ/d)		Protein g/d		Iron mg/d	
	Males	Females				
0–3 mths	545 (2.28)	515 (2.16)	—		1.3	
4–6 mths	690 (2.89)	645 (2.69)	10.6		3.3	
7–9 mths	825 (3.44)	765 (3.20)	11.0		6.0	
10–12 mths	920 (3.85)	865 (3.61)	11.2		6.0	
1–3 yrs	1230 (5.15)	1165 (4.86)	11.7		5.3	
4–6 yrs	1715 (7.16)	1545 (6.46)	14.8		4.7	
7–10 yrs	1970 (8.24)	1740 (7.28)	22.8		6.7	
			Males	Females	Males	Females
11–14 yrs	2220 (9.27)	1845 (7.92)	33.8	33.1	8.7	11.4*
15–18 yrs	2755 (11.51)	2110 (8.83)	46.1	37.1	8.7	11.4*
19–50 yrs	2550 (10.60)	1940 (8.10)	44.4	36.0	6.7	11.4*
51–59 yrs	2550 (10.60)	1900 (8.00)	42.6	37.2	6.7	6.7
60–64 yrs	2380 (9.93)	1900 (7.99)	42.6	37.2	6.7	6.7
65–74 yrs	2330 (9.71)	1900 (7.96)	42.6	37.2	6.7	6.7
75+yrs	2100 (8.77)	1810 (7.61)	42.6	37.2	6.7	6.7

* About 10% of women with very high menstrual losses will require more iron than shown.
Source: Balmforth, H., *A Chef's Guide to Nutrition* (Cambridge University Press, 1991). More detailed tables for all the nutrients will be found in *Dietary Reference Values for Food, Energy and Nutrients for the United Kingdom.* Report on Health and Social Subjects 41, HMSO 1991, on which the above table is based.

finish a meal, and though it will probably contain some vitamins and minerals, it will have little vitamin C compared with strawberries, blackcurrants and oranges. So, though pleasant to eat and satisfying to our appetite, a piece of cake may be nutritionally inadequate to our needs if we have not obtained sufficient vitamin C from other sources.

Set menus, however, need to fulfil the nutritional needs of the clientele. Different customers will have different requirements, as nutrition is dependent on sex, age and how active the individual is. Manual workers will need a diet higher in energy-giving foods than sedentary office workers; adults require less body-building protein than growing children. Table 3.5 shows some of the dietary reference values (DRVs) for food energy and nutrients for different ages. Dietary reference values are new guidelines introduced to replace the RDI, or recommended daily intake, of nutrients. DRV tables show the estimated average requirement (EAR) for most people's needs of the following:

the major nutrients, that is proteins, fats, sugars, starches, vitamins and minerals;
dietary fibre (or non-starch polysaccharides);
energy.

Special diets are often required in institutions. For example, patients in hospital may be unable to eat certain foods because of allergies or illness. The caterer also has to provide a nutritionally balanced meal for vegetarians and vegans, who do not eat meat. Other sources of protein must be provided for them to choose from.

To enable the caterer and the health-conscious to plan nutritionally balanced menus, foods have been analysed for the quantity and types of nutrient they contain. (See Table 3.6.) A caterer can check the nutrient content of average-sized portions of foods to be included in a menu, and then supplement them with foods containing any missing nutrients. Table 3.7 shows the nutrient breakdown for an average portion of shepherd's pie. If this was to be the only meal that day, then it would provide insufficient nutrients to meet the consumer's needs. By including other food items in the meal, the missing nutrients can be supplied.

Table 3.6 **Energy in food**

Food (1 helping)	Energy (kJ)	Protein (g)	Carbohydrate (g)	Fat (g)
Grapefruit (half)	92	1	5	0
Sugar (spoonful)	188	0	12	0
Breakfast cereals (with milk)				
Corn Flakes	1403	10	60	8
Weetabix	1274	12	49	9
Rice Krispies	1274	9	53	9
Porridge	728	7	18	9
Cooked breakfast				
Bacon (rasher)	1132	6	0	27
Kipper	922	19	0	16
Boiled egg	376	7	0	7
Fried egg	504	7	0	10
Buttered toast	393	2	16	3
Preserves (for one slice of bread or toast)				
Honey	172	0	11	0
Jam or marmalade	155	0	10	0
Golden syrup	176	0	11	0
Drinks (one cup or glass)				
Tea with milk	54	1	1	0
Coffee with milk	72	1	2	2
Drinking chocolate (made with milk)	636	7	15	8
Milk	539	6	10	8
Sugar (teaspoon)	94	0	6	0
Fruit juice (pure)	394	2	23	0
Snacks				
1 slice of buttered bread	393	2	16	3
Ham (slice)	250	2	0	6
Cheese (slice)	245	4	0	5
Fish finger	342	6	9	3
Sausage	439	3	3	9
Meat pattie	558	5	10	6
Beefburger	660	5	5	13
Fishcake	510	9	14	5
Meat samosa	512	5	16	6
Sardine	224	4	0	4
Tomato soup	400	2	14	5
Meat				
Pork chop	3762	32	0	86
Lamb chop	1596	15	0	34
Fried liver	1156	30	4	16
Steak	1014	29	0	14
Beef curry	1250	26	1	22
Roast lamb	1190	25	0	20
Roast pork	1344	25	0	23
Roast beef	1050	27	0	15

Food (1 helping)	Energy (kJ)	Protein (g)	Carbohydrate (g)	Fat (g)
Meat pie	2166	23	28	36
Chicken (quarter)	1542	59	0	15
Fish				
Fried cod	834	20	8	10
Poached fish	492	27	0	1
Tinned salmon	557	20	0	6
Vegetables (cooked)				
Chips	1405	6	53	13
Boiled potatoes	331	1	20	0
Roast potatoes	515	3	27	2
Baked beans	385	6	17	0
Garden peas	102	3	4	0
Mushy peas	201	4	9	0
Sprouts	67	2	2	0
Cabbage	34	1	1	0
Carrots	96	1	5	0
Cauliflower	101	3	3	0
Vegetable stir fry	500	5	20	10
Rice, pasta and dough				
Rice	854	4	49	1
Spaghetti	864	6	48	1
Chapatti	1500	19	20	0
Yoghurt				
Natural	335	5	8	4
Fruit	460	5	19	3
Fresh fruit				
Apple	220	0	14	0
Orange	252	1	14	0
Banana	540	2	33	0
Puddings, cakes and sweets				
Fresh raspberries	105	1	6	0
Fresh strawberries	109	1	6	0
Tinned apricots	444	1	28	0
Tinned peaches	369	0	23	0
Tinned pineapple	318	0	20	0
Apple pie	2462	6	81	29
Single cream	225	1	1	5
Custard	867	6	31	8
Ice cream	805	4	20	11
Currant bun	1374	8	59	9
Fruit cake	3084	9	110	32
Plain cake	2703	11	75	36
Jam tart	1638	3	68	14
Rice pudding	595	4	16	8
Chocolate bar (100 g)	2422	9	55	38

Table 3.7 Nutritional value of shepherd's pie (4 portions)

| | Energy value | | Nutrient content | | | | | | | | | | | |
	kcal	kJ	water (g)	protein (g)	fat (g)	carbo-hydrate (g)	calcium (mg)	iron (mg)	vit A (µg)	vit D (µg)	B_1 thiamin (mg)	B_2 riboflavin (mg)	niacin (mg)	vit C (mg)
250 g raw beef	550.0	2300.0	172.5	47.5	40.0	0	0	6.75	0	0	0.15	0.75	10.0	0
50 g raw onion	12.5	50.0	47.0	0.5	0	2.5	15.0	0.15	0	0	0.02	0.03	0	0.5
12.5 g dripping	111.25	471.25	0.01	0	12.5	0	0	0	0	0	0	0	0	0
12.5 g flour	42.5	177.5	1.0	1.38	0.15	9.4	5.0	0.25	0	0	0.04	0	0.25	0
250 ml water	0	0	250.0	0	0	0	0	0	0	0	0	0	0	0
salt, pepper	0	0	0	0	0	0	0	0	0	0	0	0	0	0
750 g potatoes (boiled)	600.0	2475.0	607.5	10.5	0	150.0	0	2.2	0	0	0.75	0.23	7.5	75.0
25 g margarine	182.5	765.0	4.0	0	20.25	0	0	0	255.0	8.0	0	0	0	0
100 ml milk (whole)	65.0	270.0	87.0	3.3	3.8	4.7	120.0	0	50.0	0.15	0.05	0.20	0.1	1.0
Total nutritional value	1564.0	6509.0	0	63.2	76.7	166.6	140.0	9.4	300.0	8.15	1.01	1.21	17.85	76.5
Nutritional value of 1 portion i.e. quarter of recipe	391	1627.0	0	15.8	19.2	41.7	35.0	2.4	75.0	2.04	0.25	0.3	4.5	19.13

Adapted from Clarke, D. and Herbert, E. *Food Facts* (Basingstoke, Hants., Macmillan, 1986).

Things to do

1 Sugars vary in their strength of sweetness. Taste the following and score them on a scale of 1 to 10 for sweetness. Give 1 to the least sweet and 10 to the sweetest: lactose, maltose, glucose, sucrose, invert sugar, fructose, starch. Now taste an artificial sweetener to see how it compares in strength to natural sugars. (Fructose can be obtained from most supermarkets, where it appears alongside other sugars. The remaining sugars are readily available from health food stores or chemists.)

2 One way of cutting down the amount of sugar we eat is to use artificial sweeteners. But is their taste acceptable?

Make up a measuring jug of tea or coffee and pour into six cups. To each of the cups add the following sweeteners in the amounts you would normally take (teaspoons or tablets):

saccharine	cup 1
Aspartame	cup 2
Nutrasweet	cup 3
fructose	cup 4
sucrose	cup 5
glucose	cup 6

Move the cups so you don't know which is which and taste each cup blind. In addition to scoring for sweetness comment on the taste. Can you tell if the sweetness is artificial? Is there a bitter taste? Rinse your mouth with water between each sample.

3 How often is sugar added to manufactured foods? Read the ingredients list from a variety of different tinned soups and beans or packaged foods, like prepared meals, remembering that the first item on the list is present in the largest amount and the last item is present in the smallest amount.

Draw up a table, based on the example given here, and alongside the name of each item write down where sugar appears on the list of ingredients, i.e. is it listed second, sixth, or not at all?

Name of food	Sugar's position in list of ingredients

4 Various chemical tests can be carried out on foods to see which nutrients they contain. If you have the facilities carry out the following tests on pure foods (flour for starch, glucose for sugar, egg white for protein, cooking oil for fats and oils, lemon juice for vitamin C) and then on various foods which should be ground in a mortar and pestle with water to make a pulp.

Test for starch

a To a sample of flour add a few drops of iodine solution.
b The amber colour will turn blue-black indicating that starch is present.

Test for sugar (glucose)

a Dissolve a teaspoon of glucose in 10 ml of water and place 5 ml into a test tube.
b Add an equal quantity of Benedict's reagent, which is a pale blue colour.
c Place the test tube into a beaker of boiling water and leave for a few minutes, with the water still boiling.
d A brick-red colour indicates that glucose is present.

Test for protein

a Place about 5 ml of egg white into a test tube and add an equal quantity of Biuret reagent A and mix.
b Add 3–4 drops of Biuret reagent B to the test tube; a purple colour indicates that protein is present.

Test for fats and oils

a Rub a drop of oil onto a piece of filter paper.
b Hold the filter paper to the light and you will be able to see through the paper in the region of the fat drop.

Test for vitamin C

a Place 2–3 drops of dichlorophenol indophenol (DCPIP) solution onto a spotting tile.
b With a clean pipette add lemon juice to the DCPIP solution and it will turn colourless, indicating that vitamin C is present.

5 Test how good various emulsifiers are at stabilising emulsions.
a Take five test tubes or small bottles (spice bottles, for example) and partly fill each, $\frac{1}{3}$ with oil and $\frac{1}{3}$ with vinegar or water.
b To tube 1 add nothing.
To tube 2 add salt and pepper.
To tube 3 add mustard.
To tube 4 add 1 tsp of egg yolk.
To tube 5 add 1 tsp of artificial stabiliser, like glycerol monostearate.
c Shake all the tubes/bottles vigorously, and at the same time, for two minutes and leave standing upright.
d Look to see which of the emulsions separate out and how long it takes for them to do so.

6 Use the tables to check the nutritional balance of some of your past menus. How could they be improved nutritionally?

Test yourself

1 Give four reasons why we need to eat food.

2 Carbohydrates are needed by the body for:
    a growth   **b** repair   **c** energy   **d** warmth

3 Which of the following carbohydrates are not sweet?
    a lactose   **b** maltose   **c** sucrose   **d** starch

4 Proteins are made up of:
    a monosaccharides   **b** glycerol units
    c fatty acids   **d** amino acids

5 The term biological value indicates:
    a how many amino acids there are in a protein
    b how many non-essential amino acids there are in a protein
    c how many essential amino acids there are in a protein
    d how many amino acids can be made in the body

6 Which vitamin is the odd one out?
    a vitamin A   **b** vitamin C   **c** vitamin D   **d** vitamin E

7 A lack of iron in the diet causes:
    a rickets   **b** cramp   **c** anaemia   **d** Kwashiorkor

8 Each of the foods in the left-hand column is closely related to one of the words in the right-hand column. Write them down in their correct pairs.

wholemeal bread	protein
eggs	insulation
butter	lemons
sugar	roughage
scurvy	energy

9 The following table gives the amount of carbohydrate, fat and protein per 100 g in three chocolate products. Which one contains the most energy?

	Protein	Carbohydrate	Fat
Plain chocolate	59 g	33 g	4 g
Milk chocolate	54 g	36 g	8 g
Cocoa powder	36 g	26 g	19 g

Now check your answers with the text.

four Digestion

When we start feeling hungry it is a signal to replenish the body's stock of nutrients. We must eat.

The food we eat contains a mixture of proteins, carbohydrates, fats, vitamins and minerals. For example, cheese contains protein, fat, vitamins and minerals, and a cheese sandwich made with brown bread contains carbohydrates and fibre too.

Before the body can make use of these nutrients they have to be separated from each other. Then the large complex structures of protein, fats and carbohydrates have to be broken down into the simpler units they are made of – amino acids, fatty acids, glycerol and simple, monosaccharide sugars like glucose. The process of breaking down food to release the nutrients is called **digestion** and it takes place along the **alimentary canal**, a tube in our bodies which runs from mouth to anus.

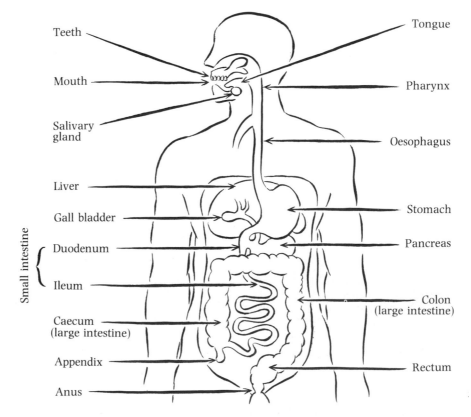

Figure 4.1 The digestive system

Even before food enters our mouths we begin the digestive process by cutting it up into smaller more manageable pieces using a knife and fork. The teeth continue the process by cutting and grinding the food into yet smaller particles in preparation for swallowing. This is known as **mechanical digestion**.

The chewing action of the teeth also mixes food with the liquid saliva present in the mouth. Saliva contains chemicals – called **enzymes** – which begin **chemical digestion**. This second stage of digestion separates the individual nutrients (protein, fats, etc.) and breaks them down into their simpler components. This process is accomplished by the enzymes.

The digestive system contains many different enzymes, each carrying out its own digestive process. For example, water biscuits are made from starch, and an enzyme in the mouth called **amylase**, which acts only on starch, breaks it down into the simpler sugars it is made from.

Once chewing is complete the tongue pushes the food to the back of the mouth and it is swallowed. It is squeezed down the gullet by muscles and enters the stomach, where it is mixed with **gastric juice**, which is made up of an acid and enzymes. The acid serves two functions:

- to kill off any bacteria
- to soften the fibres in meat

The enzymes work on the proteins and break them down into amino acids.

The mixed food, which is now called **chyme**, is squeezed out of the stomach into a six-metre-long tube called the **small intestine**. The first part is just 25 cm long and is called the **duodenum**. Once inside the duodenum the chyme is mixed with:

- pancreatic juice made by the pancreas
- bile made by the liver and stored in the gall bladder
- intestinal juice made by the cells lining the intestine

Bile neutralises the acidity created by the stomach and also acts as an emulsifier, breaking down fats into tiny droplets. Both pancreatic and intestinal juice contain a wide range of enzymes which act on all categories of nutrients.

As the food moves out of the short duodenum it enters the **ileum**, where the broken-down nutrients pass across the lining of the small intestine into the bloodstream to be carried around the body. By the time the food reaches the end of the small intestine all the useful substances have been removed except for water and some minerals.

The food now enters the **large intestine**, where water and the remaining minerals are removed. The dried-out remains are stored as faeces in the **rectum** to be passed out eventually through the **anus**. The faeces consist mainly of dead cells and indigestible fibre. It is fibre which absorbs water and swells, adding bulk to food in the intestine and providing the muscles with something to squeeze on. This speeds up the passage of food through the system. If its passage is slow, too much water is drawn out and the faeces become dry and difficult to pass out through the anus. This condition is called constipation.

Recent research has suggested that fibre may absorb harmful substances which could cause cancer and may even absorb cholesterol, thereby reducing the risk of heart disease. (See Chapter 3.)

Things to do

1 Rinse your mouth out with water and then chew a plain water biscuit. At first the taste will be bland but if you continue chewing and mixing the biscuit with saliva the taste will change. What do you taste? The enzyme amylase is working on the starch in the biscuit, breaking it down into the substances that it is made from (see text).

2 You can take the above investigation further by mixing a crushed water biscuit with *artificial* saliva (a preparation of α-amylase enzyme dissolved in water) in a dish and taking samples at intervals to test for starch with iodine solution. (See Chapter 3: Things to do.) Eventually the iodine solution will not change from amber to blue-black as all the starch will have been broken down into sugar.

3 Using available magazines and books, find out more about the role played by fibre in digestion.

Test yourself

1 On a separate piece of paper draw a diagram of the digestive system, using the figure on page 42 as a guide. Now, without looking at the book, label as many parts as you can.

2 Fill in the blanks with the appropriate answer:

Where broken-down nutrients pass into the bloodstream from the gut: _____
Where food is mixed with gastric juice: _____
Where faeces pass out from the body: _____
A gland which makes juice to mix with chyme in the small intestine: _____
Where mechanical digestion takes place: _____
Where water and the remaining minerals are removed: _____
Where bile is stored: _____
The organ that makes bile: _____

Now check your answers with the text.

The effect of heat on food

Very few foods are eaten raw – most are heated at some time during preparation to cook them. There are exceptions: salad vegetables; steak tartare – raw chopped beefsteak often served with a raw egg; and sashimi – a Japanese dish of thin slices of raw fish accompanied by a selection of sauces.

Foods are cooked for a number of reasons:

- to kill bacteria – *Salmonella* in poultry and eggs and various bacteria transferred when handling food
- to destroy toxins left on food by bacteria – toxins produced by *Clostridium botulinum*, for example
- to make food look 'good enough to eat' and make our gastric juices flow
- to improve the taste by producing cooking juices that have been squeezed out on heating
- to make the food easier to digest by softening the fibrous part – compare raw and cooked carrots

There are three main methods used to cook food:

- the **dry method**: roasting, grilling, frying
- the **moist method**: stewing, boiling, steaming, pressure cooking, poaching
- the **combination method**: braising, in which dry and moist methods work together

An understanding of what happens to plant and animal foods as they are cooked helps in choosing the correct cooking method. It may also help us avoid overcooking the food.

Vegetable foods

Many vegetables are delicious eaten raw – crudités (grated raw carrot, thin strips of pepper, etc.) and salads, for example. The purpose of cooking vegetables is to aid their digestibility and develop their flavour. Cooking will also destroy toxic compounds, like taking the sting out of nettles, and making nettle soup a possibility.

Vegetables are made up of tiny cells which contain nutrients. Surrounding each cell there is a wall made of a carbohydrate called **cellulose**. Our bodies are unable to digest cellulose and so it passes through our digestive system as fibre or the roughage part of our diet (see Chapter 3).

The nutrients that our bodies need from vegetables are locked away inside the plant cell walls. We can use our teeth to break open some of the walls but a more efficient process is to cook the vegetables. The length of time we cook them depends on the amount of cellulose they contain. Leafy vegetables like spinach tend to contain more water and less cellulose than harder root vegetables like carrots, so they need a shorter cooking time.

The plant cells are held together by another indigestible carbohydrate called **pectin**. (Fruits rich in pectin are ideal for jam-making as it is the pectin which causes the jam to set.) Pectin dissolves in water during the cooking process, allowing the cells to separate and so softening the whole vegetable.

Gluten is the protein found in flour. The kneading and rising process in the making of bread forms the gluten into a framework of fine threads which trap air and starch grains. On heating, the gluten coagulates and sets, maintaining the light airy texture of the baked bread.

The process of gelatinisation

Another important process, called **gelatinisation**, takes place when cooking vegetables like potatoes that are high in starch. Starch is present in all plant cells in the form of tiny grains and is especially abundant in the cells of potatoes. Uncooked starchy foods are difficult to digest because the grains are enclosed inside the cell walls. Cooking in water softens the cell walls, allowing water to enter the cell and gelatinisation to take place.

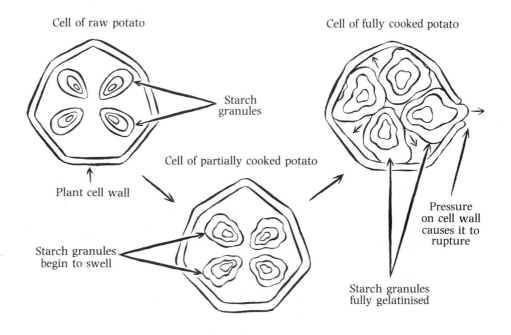

Figure 5.1   The process of gelatinisation of starch

As starch is a polysaccharide it does not dissolve in water. Instead, the starch grains soak up water and swell, but the temperature of the water must be nearly 60 °C for this to happen. If the water is heated further, by the time it reaches 85 °C the grains will have swollen to five times their original size and will have started to fuse together. This is the process of gelatinisation. The plant cell wall is unable to contain the swollen starch grains and ruptures, allowing the starch and other nutrients to flow out of the cell. Overcooked potatoes 'fall' when the gelatinisation process goes too far – all the cells release their starch and the potato structure is destroyed.

When the gelatinised starch cools it sets into a **gel**. It is this gel which allows food to be moulded. Corn flour is almost pure starch, and when moistened, heated, and allowed to cool, it will gel and take on the shape of a mould. Using this method, and with suitable flavourings added, a blancmange is made.

The effects of acids and alkalis

Fruit and vegetables contain a variety of different pigments which give them their characteristic colours. These pigments are sensitive to acids and alkalis and may change colour if conditions change. When plant foods are heated in water they release acids which dissolve in the cooking water and make it acidic. The degree of acidity will depend on how hard or soft the water is and the length of cooking time, and it has an effect on the final colour of the cooked vegetable.

For example, the green colour of vegetables becomes dull green in acid conditions and bright green in alkaline conditions. To keep a bright green colour bicarbonate of soda is sometimes added to the cooking liquid to preserve the alkalinity and so prevent the change to an unappetising dull green. Unfortunately, bicarbonate of soda greatly increases the rate of destruction of vitamin C and this lowers the nutritive value of the vegetable.

Another example is the red/blue colour of red cabbage and plums that become red in acid conditions and blue in alkaline conditions, and the yellow colour of potatoes and onions will become orange if cooked in alkaline water. A knowledge of the acidity or alkalinity of the water in your area is essential to avoid discoloured vegetables. In general, if your water is hard then it is alkaline and if it is soft it is acidic. A squeeze of lemon juice to neutralise very alkaline water, or cooking vegetables with the lid off to release acids produced on cooking will help to compensate for the alkalinity or acidity of the water.

Flavours

Vegetables and fruits may have very delicate flavours. These are usually produced by tiny amounts of different substances within the food, some of which easily vapourise and are lost in the steam. Others either dissolve or break down on heating. Some vegetables have a high sulphur content and this is released on cooking – hydrogen sulphide, the characteristic smell of bad eggs, is released on cooking cabbage. Overcooking increases the amount of sulphur-containing substances that are released and contributes to the unpleasant taste and smell of overcooked cabbage.

Vitamin content

One of the most important nutrients which is highly sensitive to the cooking process is vitamin C. It is destroyed by heating and as a result much is lost both during cooking and while keeping food hot afterwards. In restaurants and canteens where food is kept hot for a long time, over 90 per cent of the vitamin C content may be lost.

Fresh vegetables should be plunged into the minimum amount of pure boiling water and cooked for the shortest possible time until they are 'al dente' and still a little crisp. They should never be overdone. This will ensure they retain their texture and shape, together with most of their nutritive value, and do not develop 'off' flavours.

Animal foods

Animal foods tend to be very high in protein and contain a large amount of fat. When proteins are heated their structure is permanently changed and they set or coagulate. For example, egg white, which is virtually pure protein, is normally runny and transparent. When heated, the protein coagulates and sets, and becomes white.

Fat

Fats melt when heated and either separate from the food – grilling bacon, for example – or are absorbed by other ingredients – as in cakes. If fats continue to be heated they reach the **smoke point**. On further heating they reach a temperature, usually 100 °C above the smoke point, where they burst into flames – the **flash point**. In addition, high temperatures cause fats and oils to decompose into fatty acids and glycerol; this is called **lipid splitting**. This also happens when fat is repeatedly used for frying, as in a chip shop. Its efficiency is so reduced that the oil has to be replaced. It is also thought that continued re-heating of oil may result in the production of carcinogens (cancer-producing agents).

Great care must be taken when heating fats to a high temperature, because fats that are close to their smoke points harm the flavour of the food and a fat fire can cause extensive damage. It should only be extinguished with a foam extinguisher or by covering with a damp towel to exclude oxygen. Never use water, which would cause the fat to spit and burn anyone standing nearby.

Meat

Meat is mostly muscle fibres and is cooked to increase both its palatability and its digestibility. It is only the tenderest of cuts that can be eaten raw as in steak tartare. Cooking meat tenderises it and makes it more attractive to us by changing its colour from red to brown, a process which begins to happen above 65 °C. The proteins begin to coagulate above 50 °C, which gives the meat a firmer texture. As the proteins coagulate they shrink and juices are squeezed out onto the surface of the meat. These juices contain minerals and vitamins which are lost to the cooking liquor if the wet method is used. In a casserole the juices will be served up in the sauce. If the dry method is used, the juices will dry out on the surface and give off the characteristic pleasant roast meat aroma, but some of the vitamins will be destroyed. Fat melts and either runs out of the meat or, if the meat has been sealed, remains to moisten it.

Meat is made up of muscle and non-muscle tissue. The tenderness of meat depends on the amount of non-muscle tissue present in the cut and on how much the muscle has been used. As an animal ages the amount of non-muscle tissue increases, making the meat tougher. Muscles which are seldom used, like loin and rib, yield more tender meat than the shin, which is in constant use.

Cooking increases the meat's digestibility and tenderness, by converting some of the meat fibres and non-muscle tissue into gelatine. This dissolves, allowing the fibres to separate easily. Overcooking, however, takes the tenderisation process too far and the meat becomes stringy. Cuts of meat like shin, containing long muscle fibres and large amounts of non-muscle tissue, need a long period of slow moist cooking to tenderise the meat. Meat can also be tenderised before cooking by pounding or mincing, which breaks up the long fibres, or marinating with acids or commercial tenderisers, which also softens the fibres.

Some meats, especially game, are hung to tenderise the meat and develop the flavour. The time taken depends on the type of animal and how much the flavour is to be developed. Chemicals in the flesh make it acidic and prevent spoiling by bacteria. They also act on the muscle proteins, softening and tenderising the meat.

Fish

The main nutrient found in fish is protein, but as it also contains a high percentage of water it has less protein gram for gram than meat. Fish is always tender and requires shorter cooking times than meat. This is because the muscle fibres are short and the non-muscle tissue is converted to soluble gelatine on cooking. Fish is 'cooked' when its protein has coagulated at around 60 °C. Hard boiling of fish hardens the texture, and should be avoided. There is less shrinkage in fish than in meat, but, as with meat, minerals and vitamins seep out into the cooking liquor. To maintain the nutritive value of the fish the liquor needs to be incorporated into a sauce.

Eggs

Egg cookery is based on the effect of heat on egg proteins. The main protein is albumen, which is found in egg white and starts to coagulate at about 60 °C. Egg yolk protein does not begin to coagulate until between 65 °C and 70 °C. This is why by careful control of cooking times the white of an egg can be set while the yolk remains runny, resulting in a perfect soft-boiled egg. If an egg is overheated the texture becomes tough and rubbery. A firmer set is achieved at a lower temperature by the addition of salt, or acid in the form of vinegar, to the liquid used to cook the egg. Sugar, on the other hand, produces a softer set and raises the coagulation temperature.

Bacteria

Bacteria are killed by heating, but **spores**, the 'seeds' of bacteria (see Chapter 7), are resistant to high temperatures. Disinfection at 100 °C takes only a few seconds, but to kill all bacteria and spores, i.e. to sterilise the food, it would have to be cooked at full pressure in a pressure cooker for 20 minutes. This, of course, would be devastating to most food items. Regular cooking, therefore, only kills the bacteria on the surface, but is important because many bacteria may be introduced by handling, and could include pathogens. To kill bacteria deep inside the food, prolonged heating is needed and the temperature inside the food must be checked with a cooking thermometer.

Food once cooked should be refrigerated straight away to slow down the germination of spores not killed by the heat process. Re-heating should be avoided, but if carried out, the food should be heated to over 70 °C.

Things to do

1 Cut an onion in half and remove one of the fleshy scales. Peel away the transparent lining from the inside of the scale – this is a sheet of cells just one cell thick. Place it on a microscope slide, add one drop of iodine stain, and place a coverslip on top. Observe under the low and medium powers of a microscope. What does the structure of the cells remind you of?

2 Repeat the investigation in task 1. This time take the transparent lining from an onion which has been boiled until soft. Compare the structure of the cells with that in the previous experiment.

3 Potato cells have a wall surrounding many starch grains, which can be stained black using iodine stain. Take two very thin slices of potato. Cut a 1 cm square from the thinnest part of one of them and place on a microscope slide. Add one drop of iodine stain to cover the potato slice and

put on a coverslip. Observe under the low power of a microscope. What do you see?

Take the second slice, drop it into boiling water, and leave for two to three minutes during which time the starch grains will have undergone gelatinisation. Place it on a microscope slide and stain as before. What do you see?

4 Investigate the effect of acids and alkalis on the colour of vegetables.
  a Take a small quantity of a leafy green vegetable like spinach and shred finely.
  b Divide the vegetable pieces equally among three beakers or pans, and cover with boiling water. Use the same amount of water for each pan.
  c To one pan add $\frac{1}{4}$ teaspoon of salt, to another add 1 ml of vinegar (acid), and to the last add $\frac{1}{2}$ teaspoon of sodium bicarbonate (alkali).
  d Simmer each pan for ten minutes and drain off the cooking liquid.
  e Look at the colour and texture of the vegetable and see how the acid and alkali have changed the colour compared with the neutral sample containing just salt.

Repeat using onion, red cabbage and carrots.

5 Test various foods for their vitamin C content using the method described in Chapter 3, Things to do.

The number of drops needed to decolourise the DCPIP solution will give you an indication of the amount of vitamin C present. Lots of drops mean very little vitamin C, while few drops mean lots of vitamin C. Remember to use the same amount of vegetable juice or extract each time. Use boiled fruit juice or boiled vegetables – potatoes, for example – and test both the vegetable and the cooking liquid for vitamin C.

Do not taste the egg in the following two experiments, as there is a slight risk that the eggs may be contaminated by *Salmonella*.

6 Find the temperatures at which different egg proteins set. Place raw egg white, raw egg yolk and raw whole egg into separate glass dishes or test tubes. Place each dish into a pan of simmering water and record the temperature of the egg using a thermometer. Stir the egg gently to spread the heat evenly and note the temperature at which each egg sample sets. Check your results with the text.

7 Repeat experiment 6, using whole raw egg. This time add a small amount of milk, vinegar, sugar and bicarbonate of soda – one addition to each separate sample of the egg. What effect do these additions have on the setting temperature of the egg? Write down your results.

8 Compare the weight loss in fish cooked by the dry method and the wet method as follows:
  a Pre-heat an oven to 175°C.
  b Weigh out 100 g of fish and place uncovered on a foil tray. Cook in the oven for 30 minutes.

c Remove the fish from the oven and when cool reweigh after discarding the container and juices.

d As you used 100 g of fish to begin with, subtracting the weight after cooking from 100 g will give the percentage of weight loss using the dry method.

e Weigh out another 100 g of fish, place it in a pan or beaker and cover it with cold water.

f Gently warm the pan and note any changes in the fish or cooking water.

g Continue heating to boiling point and then simmer for five minutes.

h Remove the fish and drain well.

i Reweigh the fish and calculate the percentage loss as before.

How do the different methods compare? Taste the two cooked pieces of fish and compare flavour and texture.

9 Repeat experiment 8, using samples of meat.

Test yourself

1 The following is a diagram of starch grains as they appear under a microscope. In the blank space draw how they would appear after heating to 85°C in water.

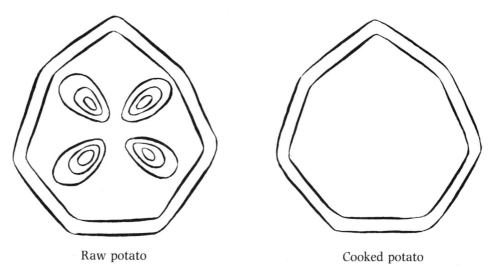

Raw potato   Cooked potato

Figure 5.2

2 A scientist carried out an experiment to find out the effect of heat on the levels of vitamin C in cabbage. She covered the cabbage with water and brought it to the boil. She then measured the amount of vitamin C in the cabbage at ten-minute intervals. Here are her results:

Time in minutes	Vitamin C content (mg)
0	50
10	50
20	50
30	50
40	50
50	50
60	50
70	49
80	30
90	5
100	0

a Plot a graph of her results.

b Suggest reasons why the vitamin C content of the cabbage falls.

c What advice would you give to a chef about cooking vegetables?

3 Match the actions in the left-hand column with the reasons given in the right-hand column.

a Vegetables should be cooked in the minimum amount of water and the remaining cooking liquid should be used in a sauce or gravy.

Prolonged heating increases vitamin loss.

b Do not add sodium bicarbonate to the cooking liquid.

Vitamin losses are greater when vegetables are kept warm.

c Cook vegetables for a minimum length of time, leaving them tender but crisp.

During cooking, vitamin C passes from the plant tissues into the cooking liquid.

d Serve immediately.

More vitamins are destroyed in an alkaline solution.

4 What is the name given to the process which takes place in starch grains when heated?

5 What happens to the fibres in meat as they are cooked, and which aids its digestibility?

6 Name three methods used for tenderising meat.

Now check your answers with the text.

six Heat transfer and measurement

We have seen in Chapter 5 that when heat is applied to food it can bring about changes in that food. The job of the chef is to use his/her knowledge of these changes to transform raw ingredients into culinary masterpieces. This is the process of cooking and the chef is seen as an expert in this craft.

Heat, whether produced by electricity, gas or solid fuel, always moves from the place where it is produced – the heat source – to a place where there is less heat. For example, if you put a cold silver teaspoon into a hot cup of tea, the handle heats up quickly as the heat moves from the hot tea into the cold teaspoon.

Heat travels from one place to another by one or a combination of methods, depending on what is between the source of the heat and the surrounding area. The methods are:

- **conduction**, which takes place in solids – the teaspoon, for example
- **convection**, which takes place in liquids and gases – water and air, for example
- **radiation**, which travels by rays and so does not require a solid, gas or liquid to carry the heat

Conduction

Solids are able to conduct heat but some solids are better **conductors** than others. A silver spoon in a hot drink becomes hot very quickly as the heat travels along it, but if a stainless steel spoon were used instead, it would take much longer to heat up – a plastic spoon probably wouldn't heat up at all.

Solids such as the plastic spoon that do not conduct heat very well are called **insulators**. A chef picking up a copper-handled pan uses an insulator – the chef's cloth – to prevent his/her hand from getting burnt. Examples of insulators used in the kitchen are plastic handles, wooden utensils (spoons), oven gloves, pastry and meringue.

The best heat conductors are metals. That is why many pans, which need to conduct heat rapidly from the heat source – the stove – to the food in the pan, are made from metal. Other examples of conductors are hotplates, griddles, skewers, baking sheets and metal handles. Pans, however, are not all made from the same metal. This is because some metals are better at conducting heat than others, but have other drawbacks – cost, for

Figure 6.1 Movement of heat by conduction

example. The following are some of the metals used: aluminium, stainless steel, copper, cast iron and combinations of these metals, or alloys.

The choice of metal used to make a particular pan depends not only on how efficiently it conducts heat but on other factors such as its cost, how durable it is and how easy it is to use. (See Table 6.1.) For example, copper is the best metal for conducting heat and looks attractive, but it is expensive and heavy and must be 'tinned' to prevent it from reacting with certain foods. Aluminium is nearly as efficient as copper at conducting heat and it is cheaper, but some foods affect the metal and it is thought to be a cause of illnesses such as Alzheimer's disease. One must consider all these aspects when manufacturing and purchasing cooking pans.

Table 6.1 **Advantages and disadvantages of metals used for cooking pans**

Metal	Advantages	Disadvantages
Copper	Best conductor of heat Does not react with food Looks good	Heavy Expensive Tarnishes
Aluminium	Light Cheap Very good conductor	Reacts with some foods Metal traces may get into food
Cast iron	Slow conductor Cheap Does not react with food	Very heavy May rust
Stainless steel	Does not react with food Good conductor	Expensive

Some foods are poor conductors of heat and have to be cooked longer than other foods. The speed at which heat is conducted through food can be increased by inserting a metal skewer into it – baked potatoes, for example. The metal skewer conducts heat to the middle of the potato and it cooks from the inside out. The same applies to chicken: chicken with the bone in cooks more quickly than boned chicken, as the bone acts in the same way as the skewer. Conduction does take place in liquids but only if they are very shallow – a thin layer of fat or oil covering the surface of a pan conducts heat to the food that is to be fried.

Convection

Place a coloured sugar crystal or a drop of food colouring into a pan of cold water near the edge and carefully, without disturbing the crystal or colouring, place the pan on a source of heat. Look into the pan and you should see the colour rise from the bottom. This is because heat rises and the hot water takes the colour with it. As the hot water reaches the top of the pan it starts to cool and because cold water falls, it drops back down to the bottom of the pan to be heated up again. You should see the colour follow this movement too. It is called a **convection current**.

Convection only takes place in liquids and gases and not in solids – boiling, steaming and deep fat frying depend entirely on convection currents. These currents cook food more quickly than conduction.

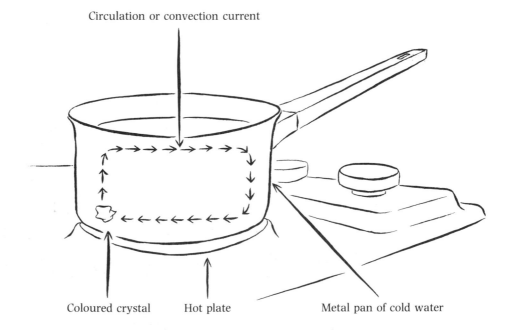

Circulation or convection current

Coloured crystal   Hot plate   Metal pan of cold water

Figure 6.2 A convection current

In the oven heat moves by circulation currents, but because the oven is closed and the heat cannot escape, the top of the oven becomes hotter than the bottom, making it more difficult to judge cooking times. This problem is overcome with a fan inside the oven which stirs up the hot and cold air and mixes them together to maintain an even temperature throughout the oven.

Heat transfer by conduction and convection work together in a kitchen to cook food. Conduction transfers heat through metal pans from the stove to the cooking liquid. The heat sets up convection currents in the liquid and transfers heat by conduction into the solids in the cooking liquid.

Radiation

When you stand at a distance from a hot stove or fire you can feel the heat coming from it. There is no piece of metal between you and the stove to conduct the heat, and as hot air rises on convection currents, it accumulates above the stove. What you are feeling is radiated heat travelling by rays – a bit like radio or television rays. They do not need anything to transfer the heat from one place to another. Grills and salamanders rely on radiated heat to cook food.

Figure 6.3 Radiated heat

Microwaves

Microwaves are waves which are not themselves hot but are able to cause food to heat up. All foods, unless dehydrated, contain some water and when water particles are bombarded by microwaves they vibrate and heat up. This heat is then conducted through the food and cooks it.

Microwaves can penetrate food for a maximum of 4 cm, so food placed in the oven should be divided into small portions or cooked in a wide dish rather than a deep one. Large pieces like a joint of beef need a longer cooking time to allow the heat to be conducted into the centre of the joint.

Table 6.2   **Microwave ovens**

Advantages	Disadvantages
Fast cooking/reheating time	Only cooks certain foods
Rapid defrosting	Limited capacity
Saves 75% of conventional cooking time	No browning
Less energy needed	Danger of not destroying bacteria if
Reduced cooking odours	correct cooking times not observed
Less shrinkage of food	Danger of leaking microwaves

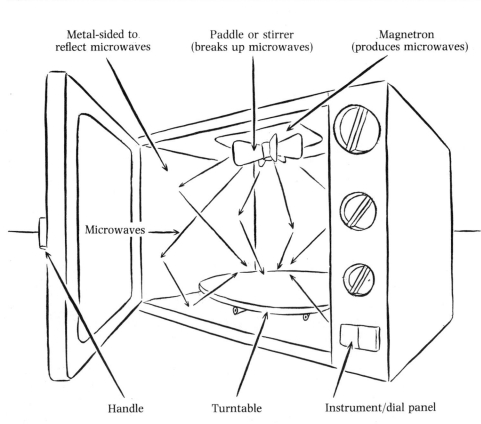

Figure 6.4   A microwave oven

Choosing a cooking method

The method of cooking you choose will depend mainly on the type of food to be cooked, though the various methods usually overlap. There are three main methods used to cook food (see page 54) and each of them relies on one or more of the three principles of heat transfer. The methods are: dry, moist, and combination cooking.

Cooking food by the dry method, e.g. frying (conduction) or grilling (radiation) sears the outside of the food and enhances the flavour. But because high temperatures are reached and the transfer of heat through the food is by conduction, the food must be thin to make sure the inside is cooked before the outside is burnt to a cinder.

Moist cooking methods rely on convection currents set up when heat is conducted through the pan into the liquid. This method is quick and allows the food to be heated evenly. Poaching and steaming are also used for fragile foods to prevent them from breaking up.

Combination methods enhance the flavour of the food as it is first seared using the dry method and then cooked with a liquid to retain the moisture.

Microwaves cook food rapidly but do not brown it, so some flavours do not develop.

Checking that the food is cooked

The outside of an item of food may appear to be well cooked – its colour may have changed, giving it a browned or even charred appearance – but this does not mean that it is cooked all the way through. A rare steak will be charred on the outside but is still bloody and raw in the middle as the intense heat and short cooking time do not allow the heat to penetrate the centre. Obviously, therefore, sight can act only as a rough guide when you are checking to see if food is cooked, but when coupled with a knowledge of the cooking methods used it can usually be relied upon to tell whether a food is adequately cooked or not.

Using thermometers

Some food items, however, require more accurate methods to determine if they are cooked – confectionery or large joints of meat, for example. A thermometer would give an accurate indication of whether food is cooked or not, by measuring the internal temperature of the food.

There are many different types of thermometer, and each has its particular uses. The liquid-filled thermometer is the type most commonly used in catering. Because mercury expands up to higher temperatures than alcohol, a mercury thermometer is better suited to measuring the temperature of boiling sugar in confectionery, when very high

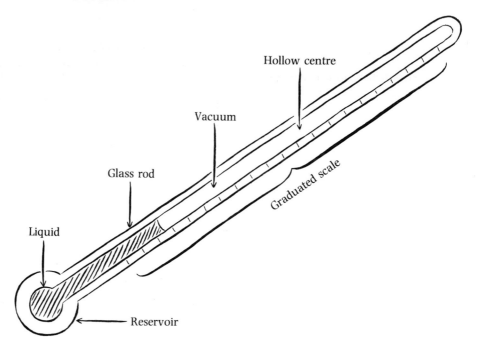

Figure 6.5   A thermometer

temperatures are reached. On the other hand, liquid alcohol can go down to much lower temperatures than mercury and so is better suited to checking the temperature of fridges and freezers.

Table 6.3   **Types of thermometer and their temperature ranges**

Type	Liquid used	Temperature range (°C)
Fridge	Alcohol	3–100
Confectionery	Mercury	10–230
Oven	Mercury	10–370
Meat	Mercury (with protective iron case and spiked point)	Covers rare (65) to well done (80); scale goes to 100
Room	Alcohol	18–21
Lab	Mercury Alcohol	−10–110

The unit of temperature is the degree Celsius, measured on the centigrade scale. On this scale the freezing point of pure water at sea level is 0°C. 100°C is the temperature at which pure water boils at sea level. The gap between 0°C and 100°C is divided into 100 sub-divisions to give the centigrade scale.

Some important temperatures are shown in Figure 6.6. The scale is based on the properties of pure water at sea level because additions to the water

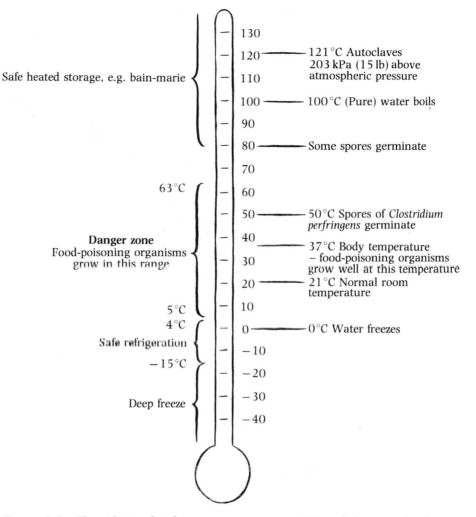

Figure 6.6 The relationship between temperature (°C) and the growth of food-poisoning organisms

or a change in altitude alter the boiling and freezing points. Adding salt to the cooking liquid for vegetables raises the boiling point of the water to over 100°C, thereby cooking the vegetables in a shorter time. Adding salt to icy roads lowers the freezing point of the water so the ice melts.

Another scale in common use is the Fahrenheit scale, which is much older than the Celsius scale.

- 100°C is equivalent to 212°F
- 0°C is equivalent to 32°F

To convert degrees Celsius to Fahrenheit multiply by $\frac{9}{5}$ and add 32. To change Fahrenheit to Celsius, subtract 32 and multiply by $\frac{5}{9}$.

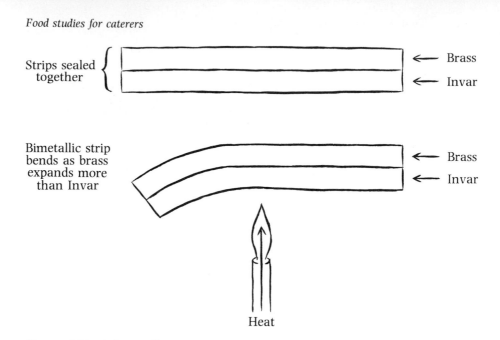

Figure 6.7   A bimetallic strip

Thermostats

Solids, especially metals, expand on heating. Because not all metals conduct heat at the same rate different metals have different rates of expansion. If two strips of different metals are fused together forming a bimetallic strip, when heated, one of the metals will expand faster than the other as it is a better conductor of heat, and the whole metal strip will bend. Metals conduct electricity as well as heat and the bimetallic strip can be wired into an electrical circuit to form the basis of a switch dependent on temperature – a thermostat. Two metals commonly used for such a strip are Invar (an alloy of iron, nickel and carbon) and brass. Brass conducts heat better than Invar and so expands at a faster rate.

This kind of switch is incorporated into oven and room thermostats, water heaters, kettles and central heating systems. Figure 6.8 shows the wiring of a room thermostat. When the bimetallic strip is straight it makes contact with a metal control knob and completes a circuit allowing electricity to flow to a heater which warms up and heats the room. As the room temperature rises it reaches a point where there is enough heat to cause the bimetallic strip to bend. As it does so, it breaks the electrical circuit which supplies power to the heater. It can no longer work and cools down. As the room subsequently cools, the bimetallic strip straightens, makes contact with the control knob and re-makes the electrical circuit which switches on the heater again. By altering the distance between the control knob and the bimetallic strip the temperature of the room can be raised or lowered.

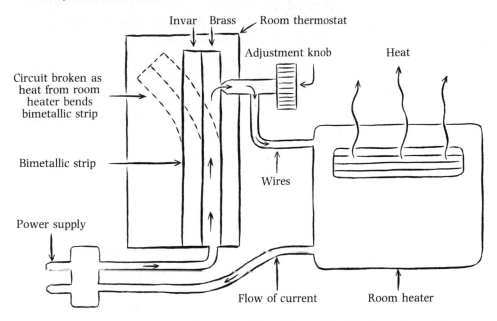

Figure 6.8   An electric circuit incorporating a bimetallic strip (not to scale)

Things to do

1 By making use of metal pans commonly used in kitchens it is possible to find out which metal is the most effective at conducting heat. Collect three pans, each made of a different metal – aluminium, copper and iron, for example. Make sure each is at room temperature. Place a 5 g lump of fat, either lard or butter, into each pan.

Using a hob pre-heated at its maximum setting, place each pan in turn onto the hotplate. Using a stop watch, time how long it is before the lump of fat has completely melted. Compare the times taken to melt the fat in each pan. Which is the most effective at conducting heat? Which is the least effective? You could repeat the investigation using a non-metal pan, but check whether glass or earthenware pans may be used on a hotplate. How do the conduction times compare with those of metals?

2 Compare conventional and microwave methods of cooking by using each to bake small cakes as follows:

Cream 50 g of fat with 50 g of caster sugar. Add one beaten egg and beat the mixture well. Fold in 50 g of self-raising flour and divide the mixture into 12 paper cases.
a Bake two cakes in a conventional oven at 180 °C for 30 minutes.
b Bake six cakes in the microwave, one for each of the following times: 30 seconds, 1 minute, 1 minute 30 seconds, 2 minutes, 2 minutes 30 seconds, 3 minutes.

    c From the results obtained in your experiment decide on the best cooking time for the cakes in the microwave and cook the remaining four cakes for this period of time. If the cakes are not cooked after this period then continue cooking until they are done and note how long it takes.

    d Examine all the cakes for texture, colour and taste. Compared to the best cake cooked in the microwave, how long did it take to cook four cakes together? How could you get around the lack of browning in a microwave?

3 Use a thermometer to find the boiling point of:
    a pure, distilled water
    b salted water
    c milk
    d soup

4 Dissolve 100 g of sugar in 50 ml of water and gently heat to boiling point in a beaker or pan. Continue heating and, using an accurate sugar thermometer to record the temperature, pour out small samples of the sugar solution at 10 °C intervals (i.e. 110 °C up to 180 °C) into cold water. Remove the samples and squeeze between the fingers to see if the lump forms threads, a soft ball or is very brittle. Taste each sample.

How does increasing the temperature affect the colour, flavour and texture of the sugar? From your observations decide on suitable boiling temperatures for producing fondant, barley sugar and toffee.

Test yourself

1 Which of the following statements are true?
    a All foods are cooked before eating.
    b Digestion is helped by cooking food.
    c Bacteria may survive the cooking process.
    d Some toxins are destroyed by heat.

2 Which of the following foods would you serve uncooked?
    a trout   b sprouts   c lettuce   d chicken

3 Match the terms in the right-hand column to the statements in the left-hand column.

heat transfer that only takes place in solids	Convection
heat transfer that takes place in a gas	Radiation
heat transfer that takes place in a liquid	Conduction
heat transfer that only takes place by rays	Convection

4 Which of the following statements are true?
   a The best conductor of heat is aluminium.
   b A disadvantage to using copper pans is that they are too heavy.
   c Very poor conductors of heat are called insulators.
   d Some metals like aluminium and copper react with certain foods.

5 How could you speed up the cooking time of a baked potato?

6 Put the following statements in order to describe a convection current:
   a Heat is conducted through the metal base of the pan.
   b At the top of the pan, water cools and falls to the bottom of the pan to be heated up again.
   c Once heated up, water rises to the top of the pan.
   d The water immediately above the base warms up.

7 Which of the following cooking methods relies on the vibration of water particles to cook food: salamandering, poaching, deep-fat frying, microwave ovens, convector ovens?

8 The ice cream in a baked Alaska pudding does not melt because:
   a It is not in the oven long enough.
   b The ice cream is too cold.
   c The meringue contains air which acts as an insulator.
   d The temperature of the oven is kept low.
   e Meringue is a good conductor of heat.

9 Convert the following °F to °C or °C to °F as asked, and write your answers in the blanks. Then match the statements with the temperatures.

Temperature	Statement
32°F = __ °C	food must be cooled below
212°F = __ °C	boiling point of pure water
__ °F = 10°C	food must be heated above
__ °F = 63°C	freezing point of pure water

10 The diagram shows a bimetallic strip from a thermostat. Redraw the strip as it would appear after heating.

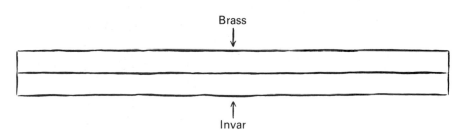

Brass

Invar

Figure 6.9

Now check your answers with the text.

seven

Microbes in the kitchen

'Germs' and 'bugs' are words used by most people to describe **micro-organisms**. A micro-organism or **microbe** is a living creature that is so small it can only be seen using a microscope. Micro-organisms can be divided into five groups: protozoa, algae, viruses, fungi and bacteria. Protozoa, algae and viruses do not usually concern the caterer, but bacteria and fungi are important.

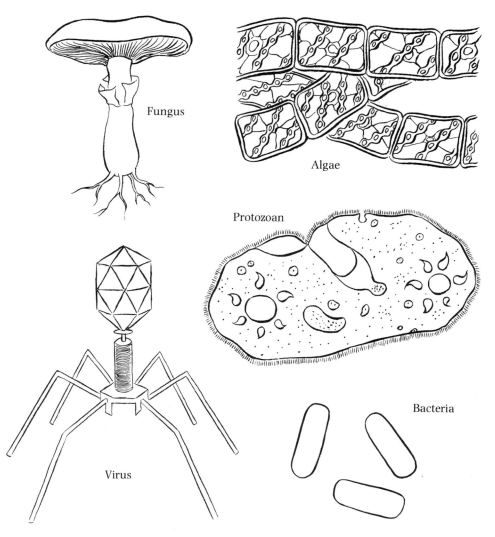

Figure 7.1   Micro-organisms

Bacteria

While bacteria are the main cause of food-poisoning and food spoilage, they can be useful when present in certain foods or food processes. Beer and wine are converted into vinegar by bacteria. Yoghurt is milk with added bacteria to thicken and acidify it and which prevent the growth of other food-spoilage micro-organisms.

Bacteria are extremely small – you could line up 1000 end to end across the thickness of your thumbnail. They can be seen by the naked eye only as colonies of millions of individuals. As bacteria are so very small it is difficult to imagine the numbers present on an item of food or even on our own skin. On a square centimetre of plum there will be several thousand bacteria; well-washed lettuce is covered with about 200,000 to 500,000 bacteria per gram.

Bacteria are present in vast numbers in urine – in fact it is they that give it its characteristic smell. Thus 1 cm³ of water in a toilet may contain 1,000,000,000 bacteria before flushing. Spray from a flushing toilet transfers thousands of bacteria onto the toilet wall so that 1 cm² of unwashed wall is likely to have 1000 bacteria on it.

It is a good idea to assume that bacteria are everywhere and every object handled is covered by many bacteria, some of which may be harmful. Fortunately for us most bacteria are not harmful, however. They may spoil food they come in contact with, but are not harmful if eaten. Bacteria that cause food-poisoning can be present anywhere and these are known as **pathogenic bacteria** and are dealt with in Chapter 8.

Coccus *Streptococcus* *Diplococcus*

Spirillum *Bacillus* Swollen end containing spore *Vibrio*

Figure 7.2 The four shapes of bacteria (spherical, spiral-shaped, rod-shaped and comma-shaped)

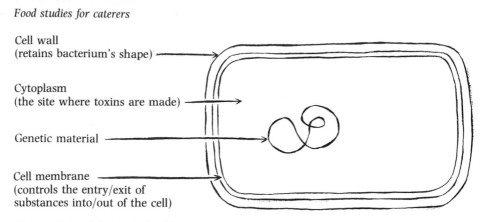

Cell wall
(retains bacterium's shape)

Cytoplasm
(the site where toxins are made)

Genetic material

Cell membrane
(controls the entry/exit of
substances into/out of the cell)

Figure 7.3 A bacterial cell

Although there are thousands of species and strains of bacteria there are
only four different shapes, which is useful when trying to identify them (see
Figure 7.2). Those bacteria most important to the caterer have either a
coccus or bacillus shape. Some bacteria are able to move with long
hair-like projections that they wave in order to swim, and others are able
to glide along. Figure 7.3 shows the structure of a single bacterial cell.

Spores

Bacteria can be destroyed by changing their living conditions – by heating
them or using chemicals on them. However, it cannot be assumed that all
bacteria have been totally destroyed when these methods have been used.
Certain bacteria, amongst them some of the most lethal food-poisoning
bacteria, produce **spores**. These are small seed-like structures that develop
inside the cells of bacteria. When the mother cell dies the spore remains
(see Figure 7.4). The spore has a very thick hard coat which enables it to
resist extremes of heat and it is a barrier to chemicals that are used to
destroy bacteria. When the conditions become favourable for growth again,
the spore germinates and releases a new bacterium cell which grows and
reproduces in the normal way, so re-infecting its source.

Fungi

Fungi are micro-organisms that cannot make their own food but obtain it
by feeding off other living or dead plants and animals. Fungi are the main
agents of food spoilage in a kitchen.

When fruit is bruised the cells in the fruit burst and release their sugary
juices. Within a day or two a furry, mould growth will appear in the
region of the bruise, indicating that fungi spores are using the released
sugars. The mould that grows produces in its turn thousands of very tiny
spores/seeds that are then carried on air currents and may land on other
food. Any food that contains moisture will encourage the fungal spores to

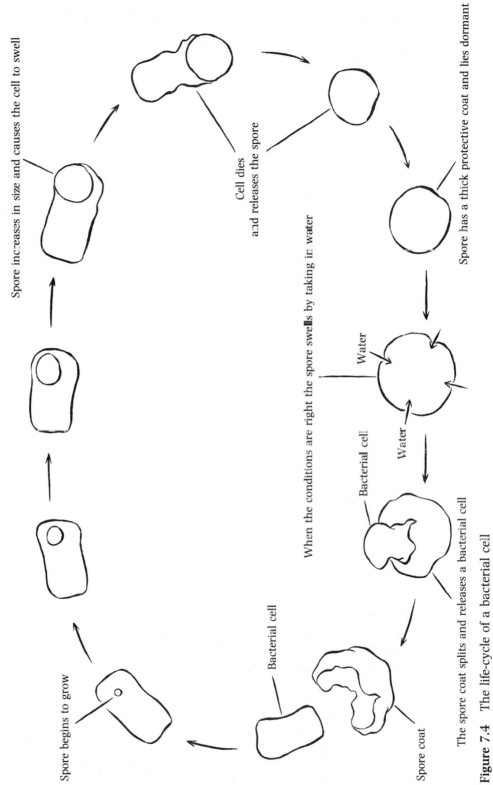

Spore increases in size and causes the cell to swell

Cell dies and releases the spore

Spore has a thick protective coat and lies dormant

When the conditions are right the spore swells by taking in water

Water

Water

Bacterial cell

Spore begins to grow

Bacterial cell

Spore coat

The spore coat splits and releases a bacterial cell

Figure 7.4 The life-cycle of a bacterial cell

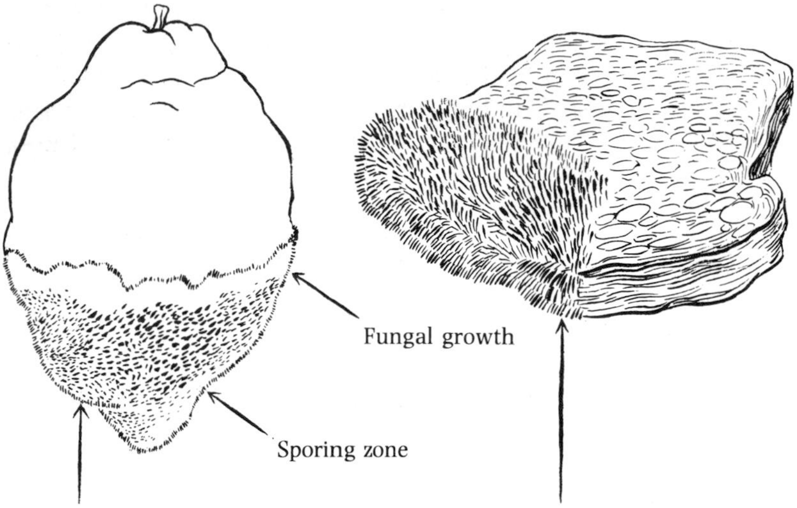

Fungal growth

Sporing zone

Blue mould growth on fruit

White pin mould growing on bread

Figure 7.5   Moulds

germinate and grow, producing more fluffy growth and further food spoilage.

Fungi as food

Many meals include a fungus or make use of a fungus in preparation.

Yeast

Yeast is the simplest fungus, made of only one cell. It uses sugar as a food source and breaks this down to alcohol and carbon dioxide. This process is essential to two important food industries – baking and the manufacture of wine and beer.

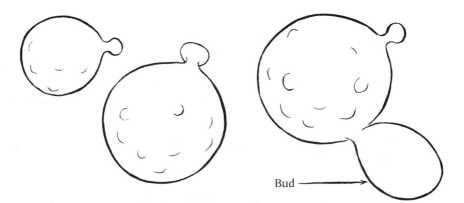

Bud

Figure 7.6   Yeast cells as seen under a microscope

When yeast cells are incorporated into a dough of flour and water, they feed off the sugars and starches in the flour and release the gas carbon dioxide. Gluten in the dough traps the gas: tiny bubbles form causing the dough to rise. The high temperature in the oven kills the yeast and sets the gluten protein when the bread is baked, thereby giving bread its light airy texture.

Alcohol, the second product from the breakdown of sugar by yeast, is used to turn grape juice into wine and malt wort into beer. The yeast feeds off the natural sugars present in grape juice and converts them to alcohol, at the same time releasing carbon dioxide gas. The latter is used to create bubbles in champagne. Sugar is added to malt wort and this is converted into alcohol by yeast, producing beer.

Penicillium
Some moulds are eaten 'live' in the veins of blue cheese such as Stilton and Danish blue. This fungus mould, called *Penicillium* (in which the antibiotic penicillin is found), grows in the holes in cheese made by piercing it with copper rods. The resulting blue-vein mould gives the cheese its characteristic flavour.

Mushrooms and toadstools
Mushrooms and toadstools are obvious examples of fungus as food. There is a wide variety of edible types, with only a few poisonous exceptions.

Quorn
More recently a meat substitute called Quorn was developed from a fungus whose fibres, once harvested, have a similar texture to beef. Quorn is high in fibre and protein, low in fat and calories, and contains no cholesterol or animal fats. Unlike meat it does not shrink on cooking and is free from unwanted gristle, fat and bone. When used in cooking it takes up flavours from the cooking liquid and retains its colouring. Its fibres can be altered to form a texture similar to that of chicken. Quorn is extremely versatile and is ideal for use in salads, terrines, pies, stir-fries, stews and casseroles. It contains no artificial additives and is an ideal food for vegetarians.

Things to do

1 Leave pieces of fruit, vegetables, moist bread, cheese and meat in separate plastic pots or jam jars sealed with cling film in a warm place for between a week and a fortnight. Examine the food samples carefully without removing the cling film. What can you see?

   When you have finished your observations make sure you dispose of the containers safely.

2 Manufacture your own yoghurt as follows:
   a Heat 200 ml of milk (skimmed of full fat) to 70°C and leave to cool to 35°C .

b Add one teaspoon of natural yoghurt and stir.

c Leave in a warm place for 24 hours, during which time the bacteria will have thickened and acidified the milk to turn it into yoghurt.

d Add various chopped fruits for different flavours.

3 Bacteria are important in the initial stages of the production of cheese. They are added to milk to acidify it and give it a sharp flavour. Once acidified, the milk proteins are coagulated using rennet to form the curds. The rest of the cheese-making process is concerned with separating the solids from the liquid whey.

Make your own curds as follows:

a Pour 200 ml of milk into a pan or beaker and warm gently to 40°C . Stir well and add 5 ml of essence of rennet. Leave to stand for 15 minutes.

b You will be left with a solid called junket. Break up the solid using a fork and note how the texture is altered.

c Warm the contents again to 40°C , stir well and strain through a muslin cloth to separate the liquid whey from the solid curds.

d Once drained, test the curd by rubbing a small piece between your fingers. Note its feel and taste it. How does it differ from ordinary milk?

4 Blue-veined cheese is really a white cheese with a mould growing through the veins. Make holes in a piece of white Cheshire or, preferably, Stilton, using a metal rod – a meat skewer, for example – and inject the holes with a pure culture of *Penicillium roquefortii*. Leave for a week in a cool, moist place. Look to see how much growth has appeared in the holes and leave for several more days if there is only a trace of mould.

5 Cook Quorn by any method you would like to try and then eat the dish prepared. What do you think about its texture and taste?

Test yourself

1 A micro-organism is:
  a a creature found in a computer
  b a creature that is so small it can only be seen using a microscope
  c a small bugging device
  d an illness

2 Which two of the following shapes of bacteria are important to the caterer: bacillus, vibrio, coccus and spirillum?

3 How many bacteria can be assumed to be present in 1 cm³ of water in a toilet?
  a 1000
  b 10,000
  c 1,000,000
  d 1,000,000,000
  e 1,000,000,000,000

4 Bacteria are able to survive changes in their living conditions by:
   a swimming away
   b turning into fungi
   c producing spores
   d hiding in food

5 Fungi get their food by:
   a making it themselves
   b eating only live animals
   c eating only dead wood
   d eating living and dead plants and animals

6 Which of the following does not use a fungus in its production?
   a beer
   b bread
   c scones
   d champagne

Now check your answers with the text.

Food-poisoning and food-borne diseases

When food is spoiled it is obvious to the naked eye. A change has taken place in the food to make it unappetising – it may be smelly or slimy, or its colour and texture may have changed.

However, when food has been poisoned, typically by bacteria, it is not so obvious. The bacteria grow on the food and reach potentially lethal numbers without any sign of their being there. It is not until the food has been eaten and the symptoms of food-poisoning become evident that the victim is aware that the food was contaminated. Although the main cause of food-poisoning is due to eating food contaminated with pathogenic (disease-causing) bacteria, food-poisoning symptoms may also be produced by poisonous chemicals or by viruses.

Food-poisoning starts in the human gut where the food is digested and the nutrients are absorbed into the bloodstream. The gut is teeming with harmless bacteria which manufacture vitamins for us. These bacteria fend off the individual pathogenic bacteria that enter our gut from time to time, but when the pathogens are present in large numbers, food-poisoning occurs.

Bacterial food-poisoning

Bacteria cause food-poisoning in two ways. Food that is heavily contaminated with bacteria produces **infective food-poisoning**. Food contaminated with toxic chemicals (toxins) produced by bacteria in the food causes **toxic food-poisoning**.

Infective food-poisoning

The bacteria which cause infective food-poisoning are *Salmonella*, *Escherichia coli*, *Campylobacter*, *Vibrio parahaemolyticus* and *Listeria*. When one of these types of bacteria is introduced onto food by cross-contamination, the bacteria grow very quickly to reach an **infective dose**. This is the number of bacteria required to cause an infection – at least 100,000,000 cells. When the food is eaten, the bacteria, due to their large numbers, survive the acid conditions of the stomach, protected by the food. Once inside the small intestine, they burrow into the lining and cause inflammation, pain and nausea. The intestine responds by speeding up the contractions of its muscles to move the food through as quickly as possible. This means the large intestine has less time to absorb water and the faeces are very liquid – the victim now has diarrhoea.

Between 12 and 48 hours may pass after eating a contaminated meal before symptoms show. This is called the **incubation period**, and during this time the bacteria are increasing in numbers in the gut. The main symptom of diarrhoea may be accompanied by vomiting, abdominal pain, nausea, fever or headaches, and usually persists for between one and three days or longer, depending on the type of bacteria involved. (See Table 8.1.)

Table 8.1 **Causes of food-poisoning**

Disease and food-poisoning bacteria	Source of infection	Time before symptoms show	Symptoms and duration of illness
Salmonella food-poisoning *Salmonella typhinurium*	Faeces of cat, dog, rat, mouse, poultry; duck and chicken eggs Thorough cooking kills bacteria	12–48 hours	Headache, vomiting, abdominal pain, diarrhoea, fever Lasts 7 days
Staphylococcal food-poisoning *Staphylococcus aureus*	Skin, nose, mouth, cuts, boils; cows' udders Cooking kills bacteria, but not the poisoning toxin	1–6 hours	Vomiting, diarrhoea Lasts 1–6 days
Botulism *Clostridium botulinum*	Soil; contaminated home-canned fruit and vegetables; poorly sealed canned meats and fish	12–36 hours	Double vision; inability to swallow, talk or breathe Fatal in 60% of cases; recovery over many months
Welchii Clostridium perfringens (was *welchii*)	Spores in soil and dust	8–24 hours	Abdominal pain; headache, diarrhoea Lasts 1–2 days
Listeriosis *Listeria monocytogenes*	Widespread in nature; recently associated with cook-chill process	May be up to several weeks	Flu-like symptoms; meningitis; miscarriage

Listeriosis

Sensational media headlines in July 1988 brought to the public's attention a new form of food-poisoning – listeriosis. The bacteria involved, *Listeria monocytogenes*, unlike most other food-poisoning bacteria, continue to multiply at temperatures as low as 3 °C.

Listeria monocytogenes are found in milk and dairy produce, raw meat, poultry, seafood and vegetables. Unlike other food-poisoning bacteria, *Listeria* invade the blood causing symptoms ranging from mild flu to meningitis. Pregnant women are particularly at risk, because infection by *Listeria* can cause stillbirths and miscarriages. Pregnant women are therefore advised not to eat soft cheese made from unpasteurised milk, as *Listeria* bacteria have been found in this type of cheese.

Particular attention has been given to the cook-chill process used to prepare meals for sale in supermarkets. In one study, for example, a team of scientists at Leeds University took 21 samples of ready-made meals from different supermarkets. Tests showed that 24 per cent of the meals contained *Listeria* bacteria. Their numbers ranged from between 100 and 1000 bacteria per gram – an acceptable level would be zero bacteria per 25 g.

It was thought that either the bacteria survived the initial cooking process or they were introduced after cooking, by poor hygiene during handling. As a result, the DSS has recommended that chilled meals should be stored at 3 °C and reheated to 70 °C.

Carriers

Some people carry pathogenic bacteria on their skin or in their gut but show no symptoms of the disease. These people are known as 'carriers' and include those who are recovering from food-poisoning – convalescent carriers – and symptomless carriers, who show few or no symptoms. Symptomless carriers may only become aware of being carriers when a food-poisoning outbreak is traced back to them after tests have been carried out. The bacterium most commonly 'carried' is *Salmonella*.

Toxic food-poisoning

The bacteria that cause toxic food-poisoning are *Staphylococcus aureus* and *Bacillus cereus*, both of which are found on the human body and are very common in the kitchen. The bacteria are introduced onto food by poor hygiene practices, like excessive handling with contaminated hands. Here the bacteria grow and produce a toxin which makes the food poisonous. Heating the food kills the bacteria but does not destroy the toxin. Once the food is eaten and it enters the stomach, the toxin causes irritation and the victim vomits to remove the irritant. If the toxin passes into the intestine it causes inflammation, which results in abdominal pain, diarrhoea and nausea.

As the toxin has already been produced on the food by the bacteria, once the food is eaten it does not take long for symptoms to show. An incubation period of between two and six hours is common – it may be even less than one hour. Vomiting, abdominal pain, nausea and diarrhoea usually last for between five and six hours, but may persist for a number of days.

Clostridium *food-poisoning*

Clostridium food-poisoning is caused by two species of bacteria, *Clostridium perfringens* and *Clostridium botulinum*. Both types of bacteria are very common in soil, and both produce spores. Oxygen is poisonous to them both.

Clostridium perfringens is often associated with meat pies or stews and is especially common in institution canteens where large quantities of food are cooked. Spores enter the kitchen in soil attached to vegetables, in meat or on insects – especially flies. The spores survive the cooking process and if the food is kept warm for a long period of time after cooking, they germinate and grow in the lukewarm pie or stew, protected from oxygen by the large quantities of sauce. Bubbles rising in a standing soup or stew are an indication that *Clostridium perfringens* is growing in it.

A large infective dose is needed to produce symptoms, as the bacteria do not produce toxins in the food. If eaten in large quantities, however, the bacteria produce many spores in the intestine, and a toxin on the spore coat irritates the gut. This results in severe abdominal pain and diarrhoea after an incubation period of between 8 and 12 hours. The symptoms usually last for between one and two days.

Clostridium botulinum is the bacterium that causes the food-poisoning illness called **botulism**. The bacterium is common in both fresh and sea water and in soil. Once the bacteria have started to grow in food they produce a toxin which is so lethal that only one millionth of a gram is needed to cause death. The toxin works by affecting the nervous system of the victim, causing dizziness, double vision, paralysis and suffocation, followed by death. Fortunately the toxin is destroyed by heating and the illness can be treated if caught soon enough and an anti-toxin can be administered. Outbreaks are not common but if hygiene standards in catering establishments deteriorate then cases of botulism may increase.

Food-borne diseases

Foods such as meat and dairy produce provide all the nutrients needed for bacteria to grow, which is the reason they are likely to harbour food-poisoning organisms. Some foods, however, harbour bacteria which do not multiply but are nevertheless disease-causing bacteria. Many infectious diseases, caused by bacteria and known as food-borne diseases, are caught by eating contaminated food. Typhoid, dysentery, cholera, tuberculosis and brucellosis are all food-borne diseases.

Some people are 'carriers' of food-borne disease organisms, but show no symptoms. Therefore it is especially important to thoroughly wash hands after visiting the toilet.

Table 8.2 **Food-borne infections**

Disease and causative agent	Symptoms	Method of transmission
Typhoid fever *Salmonella typhii*	Mild fever, headaches, muscle ache and pain, loss of appetite, nausea, sore throat, constipation, some diarrhoea	Areas of poor sanitation and poor personal hygiene; in milk, water, food; spread by excreta
Paratyphoid *Salmonella paratyphi*	As above but milder symptoms	

Dysentery
  Amoebic
 	
  Bacterial
    Shigella
	Abdominal cramp, fever, chills, diarrhoea, headache, nausea, dehydration, prostration	Cross-contamination by man in milk, beans, potatoes, tuna, shrimps

Cholera *Vibro cholerae* (mainly Asia)	Very weak, profusion of watery diarrhoea	Poor personal hygiene and poor sanitation
Brucellosis *Brucella abortis*	Fever, headache, sweating, joint pains	Infected milk of cattle, sheep, goats
Tuberculosis *Mycobacterium tuberculosis*	Mainly affects the lungs	Untreated raw milk
Campylobacter enteritis (diarrhoea) *Campylobacter jejuni*	Flu-like symptoms and fever, headaches, general aches, diarrhoea, abdominal cramps	Untreated raw milk

Milk-borne diseases

Milk is an ideal food source for bacteria. It has a lot of water, protein, carbohydrates and has a neutral pH, i.e. it is neither acid nor alkaline. Almost all milk-borne diseases come from raw (untreated) milk and cheese. The sale of raw milk has been banned in Scotland since 1980.

The bacteria present in milk may come from the cow, from human handling or from the soil. The number of bacteria present in the milk will depend on the standards of hygiene used during milking and processing. Farmers are paid incentives to improve their standards of hygiene during milking. The fewer the number of bacteria found in samples of a farmer's milk, the more the farmer is paid for it.

Diseases carried in milk include tuberculosis, brucellosis, typhoid and dysentery. *Staphylococcus*, *Salmonella* and *Campylobacter* bacteria are carried in milk. Fortunately all but *Salmonella* and *Campylobacter* are rare, but these two bacteria are on the increase.

Heat treatment of milk

Heat treatment is used to remove bacteria from milk. All methods of heat treatment change the taste of the milk to some degree. Each treatment varies in the number of bacteria it destroys. Only by drinking unpasteurised milk 'straight from the cow' can one get the real taste of milk. However, care must be taken to select a dairy with high standards of hygiene to supply the milk. Raw milk does not keep as long as milk that has been processed.

In addition to untreated, raw milk there are three other types of milk available, each of which has undergone some form of heat treatment. This treatment removes bacteria altogether or reduces their numbers. The three types of treated milk are pasteurised milk, sterilised milk, and ultra-high-temperature milk (UHT).

Pasteurisation   Originally milk was treated in batches and heated to between 63 and 65 °C for 30 minutes. It was stirred constantly and then rapidly cooled to below 10 °C. This method is called **low-temperature-long-holding pasteurisation**. A more modern process is termed **high-temperature-short-holding pasteurisation** and is a continuous process. Milk is pumped along a short pipe and heated to 72 °C for 15 seconds. Then as it flows along the pipe it is cooled to below 10 °C.

Pasteurisation does not appreciably alter the taste of the milk. It kills the pathogenic bacteria but does not kill all of the bacteria present in the milk. Because the total number of bacteria is reduced the milk keeps longer – two days at room temperature and three to four days in the fridge. Spores of *Bacillus cereus* are not killed by pasteurisation. They can germinate and cause 'bitty cream' in hot tea. Germination occurs within hours at room temperature; growth of the new bacterial cell can only be slowed by refrigeration.

Sterilisation   Sterilisation kills all bacteria present in milk. The milk is put in bottles and then heated in steam to over 104 °C for 20 minutes to destroy the bacteria, but at the same time the flavour is altered. Sterilised milk will keep for several weeks.

Ultra-high-temperature (UHT)   In this process milk is exposed to a very high temperature (132 °C) for at least one second. This results in less change in taste and a prolonged storage time – up to six months at room temperature. However, longer storage results in an appreciable change in taste.

Worms and viruses

In addition to carrying bacteria, food can harbour other disease-causing organisms such as tapeworms and hepatitis virus particles. (See Table 8.3.)

Table 8.3 **Diseases caused by worms and viruses**

Disease-causing agent and source	Symptoms and prevention
Worms Trichinella worms burrow into walls of the small intestine and muscles Worms found in meat, especially pork, cause trichinosis	Similar to food-poisoning with additional soreness and swelling, leading to paralysis Lasts 7 to 8 months Prevention by thorough cooking of meat; freezing kills the worms
Beef tapeworm – head has suckers which enable it to attach to gut lining; can live for up to 25 years in the gut and grow to over 40 feet long	Slight abdominal discomfort; loss of weight Prevention by thorough cooking of meat
Pork tapeworm – a dangerous parasite that can grow into muscles (e.g. heart and lungs) and brain, eyes	Loss of weight; depending on site of attachment, can lead to malfunctioning of organs Prevention by thorough cooking of meat
Viruses Hepatitis A or infectious jaundice Found in shellfish contaminated with raw sewage	Attacks liver, causing jaundice Viruses are killed by boiling for 5 minutes

Poisons

Some poisons have an immediate effect – a poisonous toadstool will produce symptoms of food-poisoning almost immediately. Other poisons build up or accumulate in the body until their concentration is sufficient to make one ill – lead and DDT are two examples.

Certain chemicals which are added to foods as preservatives or occur naturally in foods in very small amounts have been shown to cause cancer. They are called carcinogens. Some examples are nitrites added to preserved meats (salamis and German sausages, for example) and aflatoxins produced by fungi growing in grain.

Allergens

Other chemicals, whilst not being poisonous, cause some people to react to them with asthma, rashes and swellings. These are known as 'allergic reactions' and the chemical causing the allergy is called an allergen. The caterer cannot be held responsible for discomfort caused by allergens.

Things to do

1 Starting at the centre of the chart (Figure 8.1) trace how the food-poisoning organisms are transferred directly and indirectly into raw and cooked foods. Now answer the following questions using the chart:

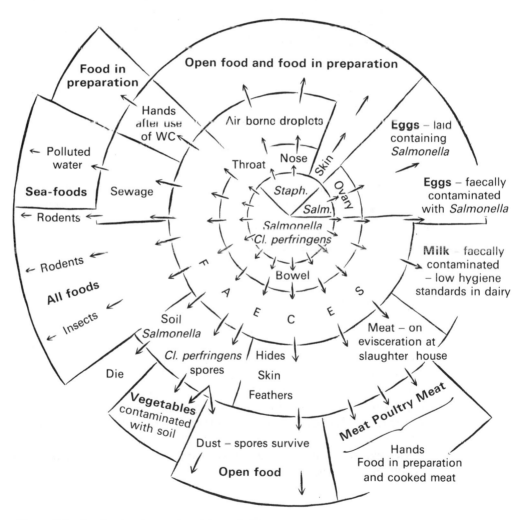

Figure 8.1 Food-poisoning routes of transmission

Parry & Pawsey. *Principles of Microbiology for Students of Food Technology* (Hutchinson, 1973; 2nd edn 1984)

a Which bacterium is found in the ovaries of ducks?

b Which bacterium is found on the nose?

c What might dust contain?

d How might meat transfer food-poisoning bacteria?

e How may seafoods become contaminated by *Salmonella*?

2 Read through the following cases of food-poisoning and using the information contained in the chapter try to decide which bacterium caused each outbreak.

THE SCHOOL CANTEEN OUTBREAK

An outbreak of food-poisoning occurred in a school served by its own canteen. The local medical health officer reported that a number of children in the school had suffered abdominal pain and diarrhoea 9 to 12 hours after eating a meal of cold boiled beef, salad and boiled potatoes, followed by steamed pudding and jam. The food was eaten without any complaint and tasted good.

The beef had been delivered to the kitchen on the afternoon of the previous day in joints of 2 to 3 kg each. The meat was immediately cooked in large boilers for two hours and allowed to cool overnight in the cooking liquid. The following day the meat was drained, sliced and eaten cold for lunch.

A portion of the meat left over from the meal was analysed at the laboratory, and among other bacteria a sporing bacillus was found. It was assumed that either the spores had survived the cooking process or airborne contamination had occurred during cooling and multiplication of the bacteria had taken place overnight. The kitchen staff were warned that boiling the meat the day before it was needed and allowing it to cool overnight was the most likely cause of the outbreak.

THE HAM SANDWICH OUTBREAK

A coachload of people left London one summer morning on their way to the coast for a day's outing. They took with them ham sandwiches cut and prepared at the public house in their home area. Before they had travelled far, many had started to eat their sandwiches. As they were nearing the coast, the first victim began to feel ill and soon other members of the party were unwell. When they arrived at the coast the illness was so acute that several people were taken to the local hospital.

News of the outbreak reached the local medical health officer, and the following day investigations into the cause of the outbreak were started. Enquiries were made at the public house where the sandwiches had been bought. The ham had been cooked at the public house, stored in the fridge and brought out day by day for the preparation of sandwiches. During this period the refrigerator motor had failed, allowing the temperature inside the fridge to rise. The woman who made the sandwiches used her hands to hold the ham bone and slice the ham.

Laboratory analysis showed that the bacteria causing the food-poisoning outbreak was also resident on the nose of the woman who prepared the sandwiches.

THE MOUSSE OUTBREAK

Eggs from ducks living in a pond close to a boys' school were used to make a mousse to be served the following day. The school cook placed the mousse in a cool basement room overnight and brought it up early the following morning to the warm kitchen. The mousse was not eaten until the evening, and the following day all the staff were ill.

The medical health officer stated that the lesson to be learned from this episode was that duck eggs should not be used for uncooked foods. In addition, foods favourable to bacterial growth should not be kept unrefrigerated.

Test yourself

1 Food contaminated by food-poisoning bacteria smells and goes pale green. True or false?

2 The number of bacteria needed to cause food-poisoning is called:
    a the toxic dose   **b** the infective dose
    c the poisoning dose   **d** the contaminating dose

3 The incubation period is:
    a the time taken to eat a meal
    b the time taken for symptoms to show after eating a meal
    c the time taken for the symptoms to clear
    d the time taken for bacteria to grow on food

4 Someone who harbours bacteria on their skin or in their gut but shows no symptoms is called:
    a a convalescent   **b** a recoverer
    c a carrier   **d** an incubator

5 *Staphylococcus aureus* causes food-poisoning by producing:
    a nausea   **b** diarrhoea
    c toxins   **d** large numbers of bacteria in a short time

6 Which of the following heat treatments of milk does not remove *all* bacteria?
    a pasteurisation
    b sterilisation
    c ultra-high-temperature (UHT)

Now check your answers with the text.

nine

Growth of bacteria

We have seen in Chapter 7 that bacteria are present everywhere in very large numbers. A large colony of bacteria can develop in a matter of a few hours in suitable conditions, following the germination of a single bacterial spore. Bacteria are able to do this because they reproduce by **binary fission**, a process in which a single bacterial cell splits in two. This method is much faster than sexual reproduction. (See Figure 9.1.)

Given the right conditions, some bacteria are able to undergo cell division every 10–12 minutes. Some take a little longer – perhaps 20 minutes. This means that from one single bacterial cell, over one million cells can be produced in just 24 hours. Therefore, a large initial number of bacteria can reach a dose large enough to cause an infection in just a few hours. A sauce containing only a few harmless bacteria at lunch-time, given the right conditions, could be lethal by the time of the dinner sitting. Figure 9.2 shows that the growth of bacteria follows a set pattern.

Initially there is a **lag phase** where the number of bacteria is quite small and harmless. At this stage the bacteria are becoming accustomed to their surroundings, growing and beginning to divide. After the lag phase there is a dramatic increase in the number of bacteria – called the **exponential phase** of growth. In a very short time millions of bacteria are produced. After this phase the bacteria reach the maximum population that the surroundings can support. As food starts to run out and waste products from the bacteria accumulate, the population (number of bacteria) goes into decline.

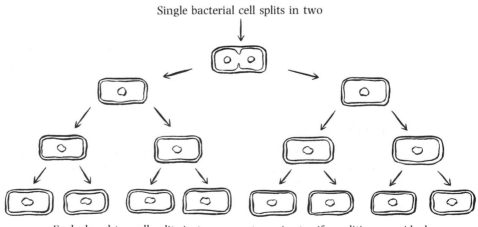

Single bacterial cell splits in two

Each daughter cell splits in two every ten minutes if conditions are ideal

Figure 9.1　How bacteria reproduce (binary fission)

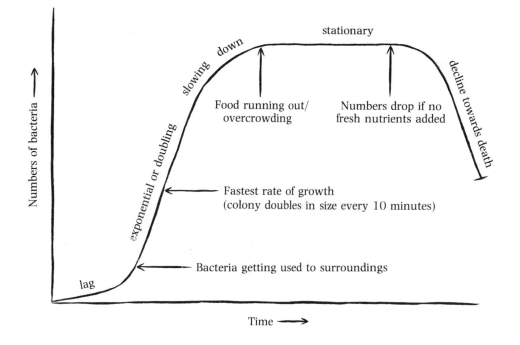

Figure 9.2 The phases of growth of a bacterial colony

The length of time the bacteria spend in each of the phases depends on the conditions. Unfortunately for the caterer, the kitchen provides almost ideal conditions for maximum growth of most bacteria, and especially for the food-poisoning types. The caterer must aim, therefore, to keep bacterial populations in the lag phase and prevent them entering the exponential phase, when their numbers can increase to a dangerously high level. A sauce kept for a couple of hours may contain bacteria still in the lag phase of growth and will be safe to eat. However, the danger is in not knowing when the bacteria are going to enter the exponential phase of growth. Just half an hour into the exponential growth phase, the same sauce may contain millions of bacteria, presenting a food-poisoning hazard. To avoid this the caterer needs to understand the requirements bacteria need to grow.

Growth requirements of bacteria

Bacteria have certain requirements to grow: food, water, a warm temperature, a suitable acid/alkaline environment, oxygen and time.

Food

Bacteria and other microbes can use a wide range of food sources, as long as these sources are not completely dehydrated. Microbes can obtain nutrition from sources other than animals or plants – fungi can even live off the plaster on walls. There will always be a food source for bacteria and other microbes in a kitchen.

Water

A cell needs water to carry out all its chemical reactions. All living creatures, including humans, can exist for long periods without food, but can last for only a short time without water. For bacteria, the water also assists in getting nutrients to the cell in a dissolved form. There is, of course, always plenty of moisture in a kitchen.

Some methods of food preservation – salting and high sugar-concentrations in jams, for example – work by preventing bacteria from obtaining the water in the preserved food. If a bacterial cell is placed in a substance with a high concentration of salt or sugar, water will be drawn out of the cell (which has a higher water content than the substance) by a process called **osmosis**, which dehydrates the cell and kills it. Unfortunately, such methods do not work for all microbes, particularly fungi, which relish high sugar-concentrations.

Temperature

All organisms have an optimum temperature at which they survive best. Bacteria grow within a wide range of temperatures and can be grouped into three categories:

Psychrophiles	range 3–20 °C	optimum 10–15 °C
Mesophiles	range 10–45 °C	optimum 35–42 °C
Thermophiles	range 30–65 °C	optimum 45–55 °C

Psychrophilic, or cold-loving, bacteria grow in fridges and freezers and, in general, they only cause food spoilage, not food-poisoning. However, pathogenic bacteria do survive cold conditions, and once taken out of the fridge they begin to reproduce.

It is the mesophilic (medium temperature: 10–45 °C) bacteria which cause food-poisoning. Temperatures around 35 °C, the optimum for such bacteria, are common in a kitchen and provide them with an ideal breeding environment.

Acid/alkaline conditions

A pH scale indicates if a substance is acid or alkaline, and is centred around the number seven. A food having a pH of seven is neither acid nor alkaline – it is neutral. Tap water is usually neutral but this may vary around the country, depending on the nature of the underlying rock and soil of the area.

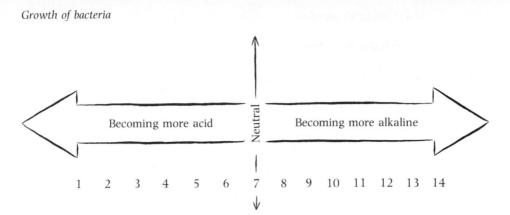

Figure 9.3 The pH scale

A food with a pH of 6 is slightly acidic, whereas a food of pH 2 is strongly acidic. Most bacteria cannot survive such high acidity and are killed. Our stomachs have a pH of 2. A food of pH 8 is slightly alkaline, while pH 12 is strongly alkaline and kills most bacteria.

Most foods are approximately neutral or are slightly acidic, and it is such a pH that the food-poisoning bacteria enjoy. Some bacteria, however, actually like strong acid or alkaline conditions. For example, they are used to acidify milk to preserve it when making yoghurt and cheese. These bacteria can be a nuisance in vinegar when they turn the acid that gives vinegar its bite into water and ruin it.

Oxygen

Most food-poisoning bacteria need oxygen and are said to be **aerobic**. However, there are some bacteria that are **anaerobic** and can live without oxygen, notably *Clostridium botulinum* and *Clostridium perfringens*. Large pans of stew or sauce which have been cooking for a long time have very little oxygen in them since the cooking process drives oxygen out of the liquid, especially near the bottom of the pan. Spores of *Clostridium perfringens* present in the stew will germinate and if the stew is kept warm, reproduce. Bubbles rising from a cooling pan of cooked meat stew indicate the presence of *Clostridium perfringens*. Reheating the stew would kill the bacteria.

Time

Foods kept warm before serving will provide ideal conditions for the bacteria on them to grow. Sauces and gravies kept warm in a bain-marie are particularly susceptible, unless the temperature is carefully regulated and kept above 80 °C.

Food stored for later reheating has had ample time to become contaminated with a large population of bacteria. Any reheating should be thorough and done at a high temperature to kill off these bacteria.

Things to do

1 Investigate the conditions needed for bacterial growth by placing a variety of different foodstuffs in dishes and covering them with cling film. Try to include foods that are high in salt like crisps, and some high in sugar like jams and honey. Include acid foods such as pickled onions, dehydrated foods like flour and watery foods such as lettuce and tomato. Leave in a warm place for at least a week, then look for bacterial and fungal growths. Remember to wash your hands thoroughly after finishing your investigation.

Find the pH of each of the foods using universal indicator paper. Does the amount of salt, sugar or water influence the amount of microbial growth in the dishes?

2 Set up an experiment to see at which temperature yeast grows best. Make a solution of fresh yeast and sugar and divide into three narrow-necked bottles or test tubes, filling them $\frac{1}{3}$ full. Place a balloon over the mouth of each bottle or tube and secure with an elastic band. Place one bottle in a fridge, another at room temperature and the third in a very warm place – next to a stove or in an incubator – and leave for one hour.

As the yeast grow they give off carbon dioxide gas which will be trapped by the balloon. The faster the yeast grow the more gas they produce and the more the balloon inflates. Compare the size of the balloons. Which is the largest? Which environment provided the best temperature for yeast growth?

3 On the graph provided plot the following results from an experiment into the growth of the bacteria *Salmonella*.

Time (minutes)	Number of bacteria
0	1
10	2
20	4
30	8
40	10
50	30
60	60
70	100
80	250
90	500
100	1,000
110	2,000
120	4,000
130	8,000
140	16,000
150	33,000
160	65,000
170	130,000

Mark on your graph the different phases of growth.

Growth of bacteria

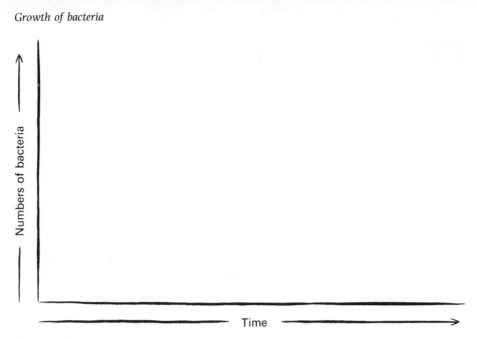

Figure 9.4 Bacterial growth rate

Test yourself

1 Which of the following statements is false?
 a Bacteria divide every 10 to 20 minutes.
 b Bacteria reproduce by binary fission.
 c A single bacterial cell simply splits in two to reproduce.
 d Bacteria multiply by sexual reproduction.

2 Which of the following will microbes not grow on:
 a plaster
 b cheese
 c vinegar
 d salted cod

3 The best temperature for the growth of food-poisoning bacteria is:
 a 25°C
 b 15°C
 c 35°C
 d 45°C

4 Bacteria that are anaerobic are:
 a unable to live without oxygen
 b able to live without oxygen
 c able to live with or without oxygen
 d unable to cause food-poisoning

5 Some bacteria like to live in acid conditions. True or false?

Now check your answers with the text.

*F*ood spoilage

Food spoilage is any change in a food that renders it less acceptable to the consumer or, at worst, inedible or lethal. Such changes can be caused by exposure to oxygen, enzymes, bacteria, fungi, insects, mice or rats. Faulty processing of canned and bottled goods may lead to food spoilage, and can be especially dangerous when the spoilage cannot be detected. Surface slime, off-odours, unpleasant tastes and changes in colour and texture are examples of detectable food spoilage.

Oxygen

When exposed to oxygen for a long period of time, some foods change chemically and become 'oxidised'. Oxidation changes the flavours and colours of the food and makes it unappetising. Fats are especially prone to oxidation and turn rancid on exposure to air.

Spoilage by oxidation can be prevented by adding chemicals called **antioxidants**, which absorb oxygen and prevent it from getting at the food. However, the antioxidants eventually become saturated with oxygen and no longer work. Natural antioxidants include vitamin E (found in fats) and vitamin C (found in fruit and vegetables).

Vacuum packing under nitrogen gas (which does not react with food) is another way of preventing oxidation. This method, however, has its problems because removal of oxygen allows anaerobic bacteria to grow. The most notable of these is *Clostridium botulinum*. To overcome this hazard, chemical preservatives are also added to stop bacteria growing.

Enzymes

When plants and animals die, enzymes in the organism are released which start to break down the tissue in a similar way to the enzymes in our digestive system breaking down food. This destroys the cell structure and makes the nutrients contained in the cell available to microbes.

Enzymes are very sensitive to heat so boiling or blanching destroys them. Freezing does not destroy enzymes – it only stops them from working.

Bacteria

Bacteria on food cause off-odours and surface slime. Foods which have a high water and protein content and little acidity – meat, fish and dairy products – are susceptible to bacterial spoilage and are known as perishable foods. These foods must be stored in the fridge, which prevents most bacteria from growing. Certain cold-loving bacteria, however, continue to grow under cold conditions, and spoil the food, e.g. bacteria in frozen fruit and vegetables. They do not produce toxins.

Fungi

Fungi are able to grow under drier conditions than bacteria and can withstand high concentrations of sugar and salt that would otherwise kill bacteria. As fungi grow they reduce the sugar concentration and thereby allow bacterial contaminants to thrive. They also attack foods that are indigestible to bacteria – fat, for example – and can tolerate both acid foods and freezing temperatures.

The two main groups of fungi that cause food spoilage are **moulds** and **yeasts**. A small number of moulds produce mycotoxins, which have been responsible for illness and even death in animals and humans. Cereals and grain are the foods most susceptible to mycotoxin-producing moulds, especially if they are incorrectly stored and the grains are allowed to become moist.

Between 1942 and 1947 during a famine in parts of the Soviet Union, people ate mouldy cereals. Vomiting and diarrhoea followed and, because this type of poisoning damages the bone marrow, excessive bleeding was also common. With body defences weakened, people contracted bacterial and viral pneumonias and died. In this way the mycotoxins were responsible for the pneumonia outbreak.

Rodents

Rats and mice are the two most common rodents encountered in kitchens. Rodents, like cockroaches and flies, are agents of cross-contamination as they walk over food and transfer bacteria with their feet. They also carry diseases such as ratbite fever and Weil's disease, which causes jaundice and is spread in the rats' urine. The meningitis virus and *Salmonella* bacteria are both carried in the gut of the rat.

Rodents are voracious gnawers as they need to grind down their incisor teeth, which grow continuously throughout their lives. They gnaw their way into kitchens through woodwork, or gain entry through drainage pipes as they are great tunnellers. Once inside, they gnaw foodstuffs, paper bags, cardboard cartons and even plastic containers. Foods should therefore be kept in rodent-proof containers.

Rodents are easy to spot as they leave distinctive signs of their visits – gnaw marks on wood and plastic or cigar-shaped droppings and dirty smear marks on skirting boards and walls.

Prevention

Good hygiene practices and rodent-proofing the kitchen are the best ways of preventing entry by rodents. Any cracks need to be filled in and hardened steel mesh placed over drainage pipes and ventilator bricks. The bottom of doors should be covered with a steel plate, leaving a 5 mm gap between the floor and the door, to prevent rodents gnawing a hole in the wooden door or squeezing underneath.

Should rodents gain access to a kitchen, they can be killed by laying down poisoned bait. Because rats are very suspicious creatures and are 'bait shy', any poisoned bait which instantly kills rats will be avoided by the other rats in the group. An accumulative poison like Warfarin, a blood anti-coagulant, is the best type to use. Warfarin has to accumulate in the body of the rat over a period of time before it has any effect so, unaware of this, the rat continues to eat the poisoned bait. When the Warfarin reaches an effective concentration in the rat, the blood will not clot and a cut or bruised rat will bleed to death. Unfortunately mice and some rats are resistant to the effect of Warfarin and so other methods such as trapping must be used.

Birds

Birds' droppings have been found to contain *Campylobacter* and *Salmonella* and their feathers harbour mites and beetles. Because of this, birds should be prevented from entering the kitchen and windows and doors should be covered with wire mesh. Psittacosis is another disease harmful to humans carried by birds.

Insects

Because insects take several different forms during their life-cycles, they are able to contaminate foods almost undetected. The adult insect crawls or flies into kitchens in search of food. It then mates and lays eggs so small they are difficult to see with the naked eye. The insect purposely lays its eggs on a food source – a piece of meat, cheese or even dried food. It does this so the emerging larvae – maggots in the case of flies – have a readily available source of food. Larvae are the feeding stage of the insects' life-cycle and they eat voraciously, burrowing into the centre of the food so that only the bore-holes can be seen from the outside. The larvae eventually turn into adults with wings, enabling them to reach and infest other foods in the kitchen.

Prevention

Once an infestation of insects has taken hold in a food store the only sure way to eradicate the pests is to burn infected foods and sanitise the store. For the occasional insect visitors, the only permitted insecticide that can be used in a room with open food is **pyrethrum**.

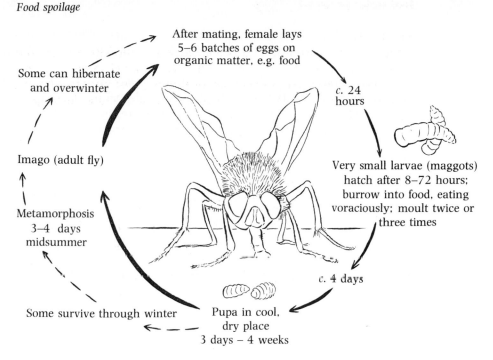

After mating, female lays
5–6 batches of eggs on
organic matter, e.g. food

c. 24
hours

Very small larvae (maggots)
hatch after 8–72 hours;
burrow into food, eating
voraciously; moult twice or
three times

Some can hibernate
and overwinter

Imago (adult fly)

Metamorphosis
3–4 days
midsummer

Some survive through winter

Pupa in cool,
dry place
3 days – 4 weeks

c. 4 days

Figure 10.1   The life-cycle of a fly

Infestation is best prevented before it becomes a problem by having good
stock rotation, throwing away infested food and keeping dried foods in
glass, metal, or thick plastic containers with tight-fitting lids.

Cockroaches

There are two types of cockroach. Both are responsible for
cross-contamination, caused by walking over food and spreading bacteria
which they carry on their feet. Being nocturnal, they are difficult to spot

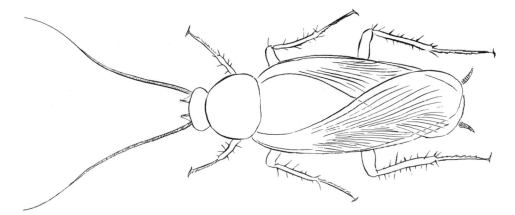

Figure 10.2   A common cockroach

during the day so a night inspection is necessary. They do, however, leave signs that they are present – look for droppings and vomit spots.

As cockroaches have a flattened body, they can crawl into tiny crevices and are often found between the plaster and peeling wallpaper. They also like warm places. By not providing suitable conditions – giving them nowhere to hide and following good hygiene practices – cockroaches can be discouraged. Should an infestation occur, then insecticides must be used.

Houseflies

The housefly is a cause of cross-contamination in a kitchen. Not only can it walk across raw food and then onto cooked food and thereby transfer bacteria, but also its feeding habits result in the transfer of bacteria.

Flies can only eat food in liquid form. They regurgitate their stomach contents onto the food and the digestive enzymes (juices) begin to dissolve the food which the fly can then suck up. If the fly had been previously feeding on contaminated food, then bacteria still present in the stomach would be introduced onto the next food item.

Prevention
Good hygiene practices are essential to discourage flies. Waste bins must be covered and sited well away from the kitchen, preferably on a concrete storage area that can be easily washed down. Bins should be emptied regularly and washed out and the storage area scrubbed.

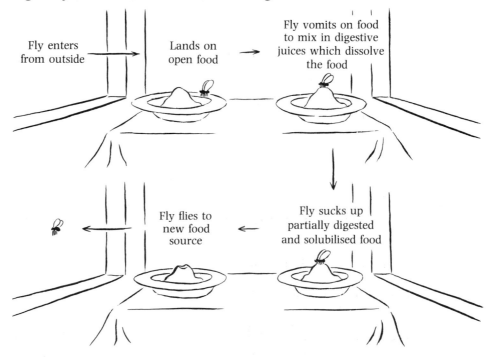

Figure 10.3 The feeding mechanism of the housefly

Any openings to the outside from the kitchen should be protected – fly mesh over windows, hanging bead curtains or plastic curtain strips over doorways. There are several methods to deal with flies that do manage to get into the kitchen. Sticky resin flypapers hung from the ceiling attract flies, which then stick to the paper. Unfortunately, when covered in flies, the papers are unsightly and need replacing regularly. An ultraviolet 'Insectocutor' is an alternative. An ultraviolet light to which the flies are attracted is surrounded by wire mesh which has a high-voltage electric current passing through it. Flies attracted to the ultraviolet light are electrocuted on contact with the wire mesh and the falling dead bodies are collected in a tray placed beneath the lamp and mesh. Although it is safe to look at these ultraviolet lights for a short time, one should not stare at them for long periods, as eye damage may result. Fly spray can be used, a pyrethrum spray being the permitted type where food is involved. Alternatively, other residual insecticides which have a lasting effect can be sprayed onto the wall.

Table 10.1 **Common pests and their effects**

Pests	Where found	Disease/harm	Prevention
Brown rats	Drains/sewers	Gnawing, fouling of food and water	Good hygiene and food storage
Black rats	Warehouses	Carries *Salmonella*, typhoid, dysentery; its fleas carry plague; ratbite fever, Weil's disease, meningitis	Traps, careful food storage, rodenticide – Warfarin
Mice	Everywhere	Gnawing, fouling of food and water	As for rats
Birds (sparrows/ pigeons)	Everywhere, especially warehouses	Psittacosis, faeces carry *Salmonella*	Traps, netting on windows
Cockroaches	Warm kitchens (nocturnal)	Faeces carry *Salmonella*	Good hygiene, insecticide
Houseflies	Food, decaying matter, excreta	Regurgitation of food spreads typhoid, dysentery; maggots	Good hygiene, insecticides, screens
Larder beetles	Bacon, ham, cheese	Maggots	Cool store fumigation
Flour mites, Dried-fruit mites	Dark stores	Faeces	Fumigation, insecticides
Warehouse moths	Chocolates, cereal, nuts	Faeces	Fumigation, insecticides

Food storage

The nature of foods determines the way in which they are stored.
Perishable foods like fruit, meat and dairy products are high in water
content, protein and carbohydrates, need care in storage, and generally
require refrigeration. Semi-perishable foods – root vegetables, brined and
salted foods – have a longer but limited storage life, the length depending
on the method of storage. Non-perishable foods – canned foods, sugars,
jams and syrups – can be kept much longer than the other two categories,
but do not have an indefinite life span.

Essential to effective food storage is good stock rotation. To assist stock
rotation, manufacturers are obliged to provide on the label a 'sell-by' date if
the shelf-life is three months or less, and a 'best before' date if the shelf-life
is over three months but less than 18 months. A 'use-by' date is now being
adopted replacing these two categories.

For good stock rotation:

- Old stock must always be used before new stock.
- On shelves and in fridges and freezers new stock should be placed behind
  or below old stock. In the vegetable store it is better to wait for the racks
  to empty before refilling.
- Supplies should be checked regularly for their 'sell-by' dates.

Failure to rotate stock can result in old food developing bacterial and
fungal growths which will rapidly spread to the new stock being
introduced and spoil it.

Low-temperature storage

Non-sterile foods spoil rapidly above $-5°C$ and below $+70°C$. Freezing is
the most popular method of storage as it not only preserves the flavour but
the nutritional value as well. The main disadvantage is that it relies on a
constant supply of electricity. If the supply is interrupted for a long period
of time the stored food will spoil. If the freezing method is slow, large ice
crystals form in the cells and rupture them. When the food thaws, the
liquids in the cells run out through the damaged walls. Fast freezing allows
only small crystals to be formed, so less damage is done to the cells. Food
with a large proportion of water is more likely to be damaged by freezing.

Open-air storage

Fruit and vegetables must be handled carefully as any wounds or bruises
allow moulds and bacteria to enter. They should be stored in a cool, airy
place on slatted shelves to allow for good air circulation. Any mouldy
vegetables must be discarded to prevent the moulds spreading.

Storage of less-perishable foods

Dried foods like flour, tea and sugar do not contain enough water for the growth of microbes, but once their containers are opened they absorb water so any storage system must keep the food dry. They should be stored in metal containers with tight-fitting lids to prevent rats and mice gnawing through them, and kept at least six inches from the ground for ease of cleaning. Lids should always be replaced and the scoop kept in the container. Never top up containers of dry food. Mycotoxin-producing moulds grow on slightly moist flour and produce a grey or yellow colour; any such flour should be discarded.

Canned food is sealed in the can and then heat-sterilised to destroy all bacteria and enzymes. However, any pinholes or leaks resulting from damage or rusting allow oxygen and bacteria to enter. Cans should therefore be checked for signs of damage. Tins left by Scott's expedition to the Antarctic in 1912 have been opened and found to be perfectly all right nearly 80 years later. Surprisingly, food that was tinned in 1900 has been opened and was edible, though caterers should be more conscientious about stock rotation!

Table 10.2   **Possible storage times for tinned food**

Time	Food
Over 5 years	Meat, fish in oil
2 years	Soups, vegetables, meat, pasta, baby food
18 months to 2 years	Potatoes, fruit, custard cream
1 year	Fizzy drinks

Irradiation

Irradiation prolongs the shelf-life of some foods such as fresh fruit without affecting the wholesomeness of the food. It is effective in dealing with bacteria such as *Salmonella*, *Listeria* and *Campylobacter* and is a useful treatment for poultry and some shellfish. For products such as herbs and spices irradiation can be used to destroy insect pests and bacterial contamination instead of using chemical fumigation methods.

Irradiation is allowed in 35 countries world-wide including the USA and France and has been permitted in Britain since 1991. It is already used here to treat the food of some special hospital patients, who because of disease run a high risk of infection. All irradiated food must be fully and clearly labelled as 'irradiated' or 'treated with ionising radiation'.

Some scientists have suggested that although irradiation kills the food-poisoning and spoilage bacteria it does not destroy the toxins left behind in the food by the bacteria. For example, *Clostridium botulinum* releases a potent toxin into the food in which it is growing. If irradiation is used to destroy the bacteria (which tell food testers that botulism is present in a particular food) there is concern that the toxin will go undetected.

Things to do

1 Read through the following checklist to see if your kitchen is adequately guarded against pest infestation. Tick the box next to the statements that apply to your kitchen.

    a How good is your stock rotation?
       New stock is placed behind old on shelves.
       Vegetable racks are emptied before refilling.
       Supplies are checked for their 'sell-by' dates.
       Any contaminated food is discarded.

    b Dried foods are kept in:
       glass containers
       metal containers
       thick plastic containers
       containers that have tight-fitting lids

    c Openings such as doors and windows are protected by fly mesh or curtains.

    d An Insectocutor or resin strip is used to kill flies.

    e There are no cracks in the plaster, and wallpaper is not falling off.

    f Ventilator bricks are covered with steel mesh.

    g Door bottoms are covered with a steel plate and the gap to the floor is no larger than 5 mm.

2 Look at the diagram and list all the faults you can see which would allow entry of pests.

Figure 10.4

Test yourself

1 Which of the following foods are especially prone to oxidation?
  a carrots
  b bread
  c orange juice
  d butter

2 Blanching:
  a kills bacteria
  b cooks the food
  c destroys enzymes
  d breaks open cells

3 All food stored in a fridge is safe from bacterial growth. True or false?

4 Mycotoxins, which can cause poisoning, are produced by:
  a bacteria
  b all fungi
  c yeasts
  d some moulds that grow on moist cereal grains

5 Which of the following is *not* true?
  a Insects lay their eggs on food on purpose.
  b Larvae eat large quantities of food.
  c Larvae burrow into food leaving bore-holes.
  d An infestation of insects can easily be dealt with using
    any insect spray.

6 Infestation by cockroaches is difficult to spot because:
  a they are very small and can hide easily
  b they do not leave any sign that they have been in a kitchen
  c they only come out at night
  d they are camouflaged

7 Dirty smear marks are signs of:
  a an insect infestation
  b a rat infestation
  c a cockroach infestation
  d birds getting into the kitchen

8 On a separate piece of paper make three columns entitled 'Perishable',
  'Semi-perishable' and 'Non-perishable'. Categorise the following foods
  based on their likelihood to spoil: strawberries, carrots, tinned beans, salted
  cod, milk, bread, jam, frozen fish, potatoes, fresh fish, packet soup.

9 Irradiation is used on food to:
  a prolong the shelf-life of some foods by killing bacteria
  b disguise off-tastes and mask unpleasant odours
  c improve its appearance
  d preserve all food instead of using chemicals
  e increase profits for food manufacturers

Now check your answers with the text.

eleven

The design of catering premises

It is important to consider hygiene right from the start when designing, building and equipping food premises. They must all comply with the requirements of the Food Hygiene Regulations (see Chapter 1).

The Food Hygiene Regulations require that:

- The siting of the premises should be as far away as possible from slaughterhouses and rubbish tips, which could be a source of vermin and pathogenic bacteria.
- Food premises should be adequately protected from flooding and built away from factory fumes or smoke, which could tarnish the food.
- There should be an adequate supply of water.
- The floors, walls, doors, windows, ceilings, woodwork and all other parts of the structure of every room should be kept clean and in good order.
- Suitable and sufficient lighting should be provided.
- Suitable and sufficient ventilation should be provided.

To fulfil these requirements certain specifications must be met in the construction of food premises.

Floors

These should be built so that they are:

- smooth so that dirt is not trapped
- unable to absorb water or fat
- non-slip
- level or sloping gently towards a drain
- hard-wearing
- easy to clean on a regular basis

Examples of suitable materials are quarry tiles, PVC sheeting, granolithic chips and epoxy resin. Materials that should not be used are wood, concrete and linoleum. The join between walls and floor should be coved rather than at an angle.

Walls

The surface should be:

- smooth for easy cleaning
- unable to absorb either water or fat
- hard-wearing
- light-coloured

Table 11.1 **Floor materials**

Material	Advantages	Disadvantages
Quarry tiles	Hard-wearing; non-slip	Joints retain dirt
Welded vinyl sheet (used in dining rooms)	Smooth sheet; coved skirting; wide range of patterns	Must have level subfloor; wears quickly; slippery when wet
Granolithic concrete (concrete incorporating granite chippings)	Cheap; non-slip	Cracks
Epoxy resin	Indestructible; non-slip; joint-free; wide range of colours	Expensive

Source: Hobbs, B. C. & Roberts, D. *Food Poisoning & Food Hygiene* (Edward Arnold, 1987)

Examples of suitable materials are glazed white ceramic tiles, stainless steel or paint. Paper should never be used.

Ceilings

These should be:

- smooth
- absorbent to prevent steam condensing
- light-coloured

The best finish for ceilings is plaster painted with white matt emulsion.

Lighting

Lighting should be:

- even, to prevent eye fatigue
- bright – ten times as bright as an ordinary living room

Ventilation

A comfortable temperature of between 16 and 22 °C with a humidity of between 40 and 60 per cent makes working conditions pleasant. Unfortunately such temperatures in a kitchen are difficult to maintain and there is no legal requirement for employers to do so. In reality 90 per cent humidity is more normal, making the atmosphere stuffy and less pleasant to work in.

Natural ventilation by means of open windows can be used but necessary precautions must be taken to safeguard against entry by birds and insects. Forced ventilation by fans is also used. Inlet fans must be placed high on the wall to avoid dust entering.

Kitchen layout

The kitchen should be planned so that clean areas and 'dirty' areas are kept separate. Clean areas are preparation areas for cooked meats and sweets and should be sited close to the servery, which will be situated near the door leading into the restaurant. 'Dirty' areas are preparation areas for raw meat, vegetables and raw fish. These work stations should be placed near the door leading to the rear entrance, as should wastebins. There should be easy access for removal of wastebins from the waste area, which should be a concrete platform that is easily washed down.

The arrangement of work stations must be such that food does not have to be passed back from clean to dirty areas, and workers from dirty areas don't have to walk through clean areas.

A staff room, staff toilet and outdoor-clothing store should be provided; these should be separate from the kitchen.

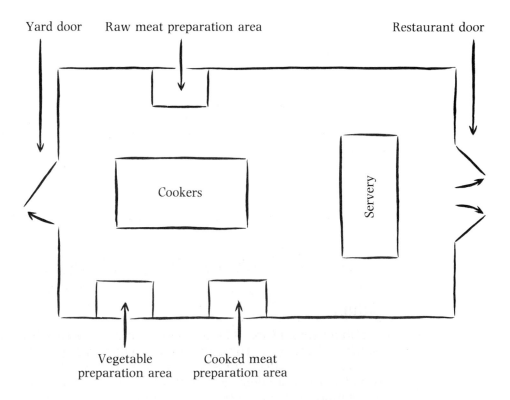

Figure 11.1 Hygienic kitchen layout

Fixtures and equipment

To fulfil the requirements of the Food Hygiene Regulations all items of equipment in the kitchen must conform to certain specifications. They should:

- be easy to clean and kept clean
- be constructed of materials which can be thoroughly cleaned
- be non-absorbent so that any cleaning chemicals or grease are not absorbed (*not* wood)
- be unlikely to contaminate food
- have smooth and unbroken surfaces
- have no cracks or crevices that could harbour food

In addition,

- rusted and damaged equipment should be discarded
- large items of equipment should have a 30 cm clearance underneath or be sealed onto the floor or be moveable for cleaning access
- there should be a gap between equipment and the wall behind.

Work surfaces

These should be:

- smooth
- hard
- non-absorbent
- free of crevices, grooves, cracks or ledges

Examples of suitable materials for work surfaces are stainless steel (the best), plastic laminate and marble, which has the disadvantage that it can crack. Work surfaces should be at a comfortable working height, which is just over 90 cm high.

Chopping boards

Chopping boards of various materials are available, though some are more suitable than others.

- **wood** – not suitable as it is absorbent and cracks; it cannot be disinfected
- **polypropylene** – the best substance as it can be colour-coded; care needs to be taken with cleaning as fat tends to bind to the surfaces
- **plastic laminate** – too hard – takes the edge off knives
- **polyethylene** – scores deeply
- **butcher's chopping block** – should only be used for raw meat and never washed with water but cleaned by salting and scraping

Sinks

There should be separate sinks for (a) hand washing, (b) washing and preparing food, (c) washing pans and crockery, as well as (d) one for washing buckets, mops and other cleaning materials.

Stainless steel is the best material for sinks and the taps should be situated on the wall. There should be a drainage surface for cleaned items and a separate stacking surface for dirty items.

Storage systems

Cleaned pots and pans should be placed upside down on racks. Other storage shelves should be made of stainless steel, and plastic wells should be used for cutlery.

Cleaning

Any dirt left behind after cleaning is known in the catering industry as **soil**. Soil contains bacteria and not only protects these bacteria from drying out but provides them with a food source, which encourages them to survive and grow. Any cleaning process must remove the loose soil, grease and

Table 11.2 **Cleaning agents**

Cleaning agent	Dissolves	Uses
Inorganic solvents		
Water	Salts, e.g. sodium chloride; carbohydrates; proteins; fruit and wine stains	Stains on clothing, especially if still wet
Organic solvents		
Methylated spirits; alcohol	Oils; dyes; grass; ballpoint pen ink	Mirrors
Trichloroethene	Oils; grease; lipstick	Drycleaning
Propanone	Animal and vegetable oils	Nail varnish remover
Detergents		
Soap	Lightly soiled items (forms scum in hard water)	Hand-washing; bathing
Soapless detergents (e.g. washing-up liquid)	Heavy soiling	Crockery; pans; clothes
Abrasives* (e.g. Jif)	Heavy soiling; stains	Bathroom fixtures; kitchen sink
Acid detergents (e.g. Harpic; oven cleaner)	Heavy fat; staining	Toilets; ovens

*Detergent powder & abrasive, e.g. dust, pumice.

Table 11.3   Disinfectants

Disinfectant	Features	Uses
Bleach (sodium hypochlorite, e.g. Domestos)	Kills bacteria and viruses; low odour	Food preparation surfaces; clothes; handkerchiefs
QACs (quaternary ammonium compounds, e.g. Task, Savlon)	Kills bacteria; ineffective against spores; odourless	Plastic/steel surfaces
Iodophors (e.g. betadine, pevadine)	Fast working; can corrode metals	Floors

bacteria. Suitable cleaning agents and chemical disinfectants are shown in the table. **Sanitisers** are combinations of detergents and disinfectants and are often used to clean pub glasses. **Disinfection** kills most microbes but will not destroy spores. It may not kill all microbes, but reduces their numbers to a level not harmful to health. **Sterilisation**, on the other hand, kills *all* microbes *and* spores.

Cleaning schedules

A cleaning schedule helps to keep track of what has been cleaned and when. It also includes the order in which things are cleaned so that nothing is missed.

Stages in a cleaning schedule

1 Remove loose soil.
2 Wash using *hot* water and detergent, which breaks up the grease into tiny particles and keeps them floating in the water.
3 Rinse to remove the detergent.
4 Disinfect to kill bacteria by use of very hot water (80 °C) or chemicals.
5 Dry by means of a disposable towel or simply leave to dry.
6 Store items *dry*.

Note: Disinfection does not kill all bacteria but reduces their numbers to non-hazardous levels.

Things to do

1 The effectiveness of cleaning procedures can be tested as follows:
   a Dust test
   Use crockery – plates and cups that have just been washed. Dust each item with white (chalk) or black (charcoal) powder, depending on the colour of the crockery item. Any grease soil will show up as patches of dust clinging to the greasy areas. Compare plates that have been stored with others freshly washed and dried. Then compare washed plates that have been air dried with some dried using a dish cloth.

b Agar sausage samples

> **Read the notes on p. 20 on how to handle
> micro-organisms before starting this task.**

Use agar sausages to sample washed crockery. Pour molten nutrient agar
into a suitable sausage mould like Viskin tubing, seal at each end and
sterilise the agar using an autoclave (similar to a pressure cooker in that the
high pressure is enough to destroy bacteria *and* spores).

When cool, cut off and discard the end of the sausage using a sterile
scalpel, and press the cut end of the sausage onto the surface of the
crockery item to be tested. Being careful not to handle the cut surface you
have just used to test with, remove the end again by cutting a slice 5 mm
thick from the end, again using a sterile scalpel, and place in a Petri dish.
Continue sampling until the Petri dish is full, taking care to note where each
sample was taken from. Make tests on the following items (all washed) plus
any others you would like to try – crockery that has been:

washed but not rinsed
rinsed in hot water
rinsed in cold water
rinsed in hot water and wiped with a cloth
rinsed in cold water and left to dry
rinsed in hot water and left to dry

Incubate the dish for 24 hours at 37 °C. What do you see in the Petri dish?
Any extensive colony growth would indicate flaws in the cleaning routine or
storage of cutlery and crockery.

c Swabbing
Sterile swabs can be used to transfer bacteria from a suspect area (work
surface, for example) onto a Petri dish containing nutrient agar. Test several
work surfaces both before and after cleaning:

cutting boards
counter tops
refrigerator shelves, drawers and handles
cooker top (when cool)
drawers (inside and handles)
handles on cupboards

Make sure you note where each sample in the Petri dish was taken from.
Incubate the dish as in the previous experiment. What is the result? What
can you conclude from this experiment?

2 Stand in the doorway nearest the servery in your own kitchen. Can you see
any potential hygiene hazards? If so, how could the layout be improved?
Now stand in the doorway nearest the outside area (theoretically the 'dirty'
area). Do you see any problems from this angle? How might they be solved?

If you can, visit other students' kitchens – sometimes a fresh eye can see problems! Do you see where improvements might be made?

Test yourself

1 Which of the following is *not* a requirement of a safe kitchen floor?
  a It should be smooth.
  b It should be non-slip.
  c It should be white.
  d It should be unable to absorb water.

2 Which of the following is *not* a suitable material for a kitchen floor?
  a quarry tiles
  b PVC sheeting
  c epoxy resin
  d linoleum

3 Which of the following statements is incorrect?
  a Walls and ceilings should be smooth.
  b Walls and ceilings should be unable to absorb water.
  c Walls and ceilings should be light-coloured.
  d Walls and ceilings can be painted.

4 Make a sketch of a kitchen, putting the following into a correct kitchen layout:
  a the servery
  b the rear entrance door
  c the preparation area for cooked meats and sweets
  d the preparation area for raw meat and vegetables
  e the door leading into the restaurant

5 Re-arrange the following into a cleaning schedule:
  a Store dry.
  b Disinfect with very hot water.
  c Rinse to remove detergent.
  d Remove loose soil.
  e Air dry.
  f Wash using hot water and detergent.

6 Which of the following materials is best suited to chopping boards?
  a wood
  b polyethylene
  c plastic laminate
  d polypropylene

7 Butchers' chopping blocks should:
  a be scrubbed with detergent
  b be scrubbed with detergent and disinfectant
  c be rinsed with very hot water
  d never be washed with water but cleaned by salting and scraping

8 Why should the join between walls and floor be coved and not angled?

9 Look at the following diagram of a kitchen layout. What is wrong with it?

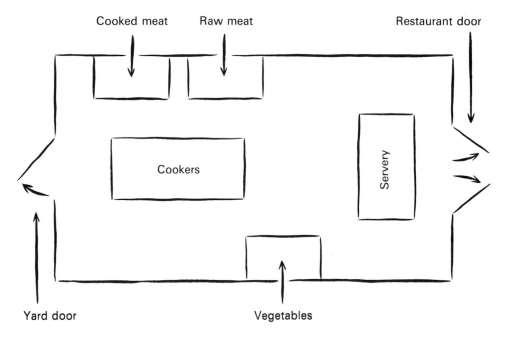

Cooked meat   Raw meat   Restaurant door

Cookers

Servery

Yard door   Vegetables

10 What is the difference between *disinfection* and *sterilisation*?

Now check your answers with the text.

Appendix 1

Food additives

Ever since 1984 when food labelling regulations were introduced in Britain consumers have been able to gain an insight into the contents of the food they eat. Since 1986 all foods carry a complete list of ingredients that the manufacturer has used, in descending order of the amount used – the first ingredient listed is used in the greatest amount, the last one in the smallest amount. The ingredients list must include all additives, listing the category of each one and the serial number that identifies it, or its chemical name if it does not have a serial number.

To allow foods to move throughout the EC, a standard list of additives has been introduced. These are the 'E' numbers. When approved, an additive is given a number which is used as part of the ingredients list on a food label. A number without an 'E' is approved by the UK but not by the EC. Substances may be added or removed from the list if they present problems or if they can be replaced by a more effective substance or a safer one.

Additives are placed in categories, depending on their function in the food. The main categories are: colours, preservatives, antioxidants, emulsifiers and stabilisers, flavour enhancers, anti-caking agents and raising agents.

Scientists and consumers have been concerned about the effect of additives on health, especially allergic reactions by the body to some additives. All foods, if eaten in sufficient quantities, are toxic, but additives are used in very small quantities. For example, $\frac{1}{100}$ g of antioxidant is added to 100 g of fat to prevent it going rancid. Many additives that are given E numbers occur naturally – certain colours and vitamins, for example.

To balance the argument against the use of additives it has to be remembered that some have given us a whole new range of healthy foods – emulsifiers have made low-fat spreads possible – while preservatives allow a greater variety of foods to be available throughout the year.

Colours E100–180

The commonest colouring is E150, caramel, which is simply over-cooked sugar. Other natural colourings used are shown in Appendix 2. Some synthetic food-colourings made from coal tar are toxic in large quantities and may be carcinogenic.

Tartrazine (E102), an orange dye, is an example of an 'A20' dye. A20 is a particular chemical structure to which a proportion of the population is sensitive. It can, for instance, make children hyper-active for a time. Other examples of dyes which may cause an adverse reaction are:

107	yellow 2G
E110	sunset yellow FCF
E122	carmoisine
E123	amaranth

E124   ponceau 4R
 128   red 2G
 154   brown FK
 155   chocolate brown HT
E151   black PN
E180   pigment rubine

Coal tar dyes include all of the above, and in addition:

E104   quinoline yellow
E127   erythrosine
E131   patent blue V
E132   indigo carmine
 133   brilliant blue FCF

Some types are possibly harmful – ones produced using ammonia cause vitamin B deficiency in rats. The number has been reduced to six, and work is being carried out to find the safest form.

Preservatives E200–290

Many methods of food preservation rely on the addition of natural substances – salt or sugar, alcohol or vinegar. Artificially produced preservatives include sulphur dioxide (E220), used widely in fruit juices, wines and jams; benzoic acid (E210), used in coffee and soft drinks; and sodium or potassium nitrate (E251 & E252), used in the preservation of meats and fish.

Antioxidants E300–321

These are a special form of preservative used to prevent fats and oil reacting with oxygen in the air and becoming rancid or losing valuable vitamins. Vitamin C (ascorbic acid, E300) is a natural antioxidant, as are citric and tartaric acids (E330 & E334).

Emulsifiers, stabilisers and thickeners E322–494

When two liquids which do not usually mix are forced together – oil and water, for example – they will eventually separate out unless they are stabilised chemically. Most emulsifiers used today occur naturally. Lecithin (E322), found in egg yolks, is an emulsifier used to stabilise mayonnaise; locust bean gum (E410) from the carob bean and gum arabic (E414) from the sap of *Acacia senegal* and other African acacia trees (members of the pea family) are commonly used natural stabilisers.

Thickening and gelling agents have a similar function to emulsifiers and stabilisers. Pectin (E440) is used to set jam. Thickeners do the same job as flour in sauces, giving body to the consistency of the product.

Low-calorie additives E420–421

Artificial sweeteners are used in low-calorie or diet foods. Only two of the permitted sugar substitutes have E numbers, Sorbitol (E420) and Mannitol (E421). Saccharin and Aspartame are the two most familiar examples of artificial sweeteners permitted in the UK. Naturally sweet substances, e.g. glucose and fructose, are classed as foods rather than sweeteners.

Miscellaneous additives

Many different substances, having different uses, are included in this category. In this group are flavour enhancers, such as monosodium glutamate (E621), which is extracted from seaweed and is widely used to develop the flavour of bland food products and make them more tasty. MSG, as it is known, is used a great deal in Chinese cookery. It is thought to be the cause of a rapid heart beat, a condition experienced by some people after eating a meal heavily laced with monosodium glutamate.

Also in this group are propellant gases for food aerosols and anti-foaming agents.

Appendix 2

*P*ermitted additives (1990)

Colours

Number	Name	Products in which found
E100	curcumin	flour confectionery, margarine, rice
E101	riboflavin	sauces, processed cheese
101(a)	riboflavin-5′-phosphate	preserves
E102	tartrazine	soft drinks (formerly in many yellow/orange products)
E104	quinoline yellow	Scotch eggs
107	yellow 2G	
E110	sunset yellow FCF	biscuits, soups, Swiss rolls
E120	cochineal	alcoholic drinks
E122	carmoisine	jams, preserves, soups, sweets
E123	amaranth	cake mixes, soups
E124	ponceau 4R	dessert mixes, soups
E127	erythrosine	glacé cherries, trifle mix
128	red 2G	sausages
E131	patent blue V	Scotch eggs
E132	indigo carmine	biscuits, sweets
133	brilliant blue FCF	canned vegetables
E140	chlorophyll	soap, oils
E141	copper complexes of chlorophyll and chlorophyllins	green vegetables in liquid
E142	green S	pastilles, tinned peas
E150	caramel	beer, soft drinks, sauces, gravy browning
E151	black PN	sauces
E153	carbon black (vegetable carbon)	liquorice, preserves
154	brown FK	kippers (will be deleted when suitable replacement available)
155	brown HT (chocolate brown HT)	chocolate cake
160(a)	alpha-carotene; beta-carotene; gamma-carotene	margarine, soft drinks
E160(b)	annatto; bixin; norbixin	crisps, butter, coleslaw
E160(c)	capsanthin; capsorubin	cheese slices
E160(d)	lycopene	
E160(e)	beta-apo-8′-carotenal	
E160(f)	ethyl ester of beta-apo-8′-carotenoic acid	
E161(a)	flavoxanthin	
E161(b)	lutein	
E161(c)	cryptoxanthin	
E161(d)	rubixanthin	
E161(e)	violaxanthin	
E161(f)	rhodoxanthin	
E161(g)	canthaxanthin	biscuits (likely to be deleted)
E162	beetroot red (betanin)	ice-cream, liquorice
E163	anthocyanins	yoghurts
E171	titanium dioxide	sweets, horseradish sauce
E172	iron oxides; iron hydroxides	dessert mixes, cake mixes
E173	aluminium ⎫	
E174	silver ⎬	sugar, confectionery, cake decorations
E175	gold ⎭	

E180	pigment rubine (lithol rubine BK)	rind of cheese
	methyl violet	surface marking of citrus fruit
	paprika	canned vegetables
	saffron; crocin	
	sandalwood; santolin	
	turmeric	soups

Preservatives

Number	Name	Products in which found
E200	sorbic acid	soft drinks, fruit yoghurts, processed cheese slices, sweets
E201	sodium sorbate	
E202	potassium sorbate	pizza, cheese spread, cakes
E203	calcium sorbate	
E210	benzoic acid	
E211	sodium benzoate	
E212	potassium benzoate	
E213	calcium benzoate	
E214	ethyl 4-hydroxybenzoate (ethyl para-hydroxybenzoate)	
E215	ethyl 4-hydroxybenzoate, sodium salt (sodium ethyl para-hydroxybenzoate)	pickles, cheesecake mix, sauces, flavourings, beer, jam, salad cream, soft drinks, fruit pulp, fruit-based pie fillings, marinated herring and mackerel, desserts
E216	propyl 4-hydroxybenzoate (propyl para-hydroxybenzoate)	
E217	propyl 4-hydroxybenzoate, sodium salt (sodium propyl para-hydroxybenzoate)	
E218	methyl 4-hydroxybenzoate (methyl para-hydroxybenzoate)	
E219	methyl 4-hydroxybenzoate, sodium salt (sodium methyl para-hydroxybenzoate)	
E220	sulphur dioxide	
E221	sodium sulphite	
E222	sodium hydrogen sulphite (sodium bisulphite)	dried fruit, dehydrated vegetables, fruit juices, fruit pulp, fruit syrups, drinks, wine, egg yolk, pickles
E223	sodium metabisulphite	
E224	potassium metabisulphite	
E226	calcium sulphite	
E227	calcium hydrogen sulphite (calcium bisulphite)	
E230	biphenyl (diphenyl)	
E231	2-hydroxybiophenyl (orthophenylphenate)	
E232	sodium biphenyl-2-yl oxide (sodium orthophenylphenate)	fruit skins, surface of citrus fruits, surface treatment of bananas
E233	2-(thiazol-4-yl) benzimidazole (thiabendazole)	
234	nisin	cheese, clotted cream, canned foods
E239	hexamine (hexamethylenetetramine)	marinated herring and mackerel
E249	potassium nitrite	
E250	sodium nitrite	cooked meats, bacon, ham, cured meats, corned beef, tongue, some cheeses
E251	sodium nitrate	
E252	potassium nitrate	
E280	propionic acid	
E281	sodium propionate	bread, flour confectionery, dairy products, pizza, Christmas pudding
E282	calcium propionate	
E283	potassium propionate	

Antioxidants

Number	Name	Products in which found
E300	L-ascorbic acid	
E301	sodium L-ascorbate	fruit drinks, also used to improve flour and
E302	calcium L-ascorbate	bread dough, dried potato, sausages, meat
E304	6-0-palmitoyl-L-ascorbic acid (ascorbyl palmitate)	loaf, Scotch eggs, steak cubes
E306	extracts of natural origin rich in tocopherols	
E307	synthetic alpha-tocopherol	vegetable oils, cereal-based baby foods
E308	synthetic gamma-tocopherol	
E309	synthetic delta-tocopherol	
E310	propyl gallate	
E311	octyl gallate	vegetable oils, chewing gum, margarine
E312	dodecyl gallate	
E320	butylated hydroxyanisole (BHA)	beef stock cubes, cheese spread, biscuits, convenience foods
E321	butylated hydroxytoluene (BHT)	chewing gum
E322	lecithins	low-fat spreads, in chocolate as an emulsifier, confectionery
	diphenylamine	
	ethoxyquin	on apples and pears used to prevent 'scald' (discolouration)

Emulsifiers and stabilisers

Number	Name	Products in which found
E400	alginic acid	
E401	sodium alginate	
E402	potassium alginate	ice-cream, soft and processed cheese, cake
E403	ammonium alginate	mixes, salad dressings, cottage cheese,
E404	calcium alginate	synthetic cream
E405	propane-1, 2-diol alginate (propylene glycol alginate)	
E406	agar	ice-cream, frozen trifle
E407	carrageenan	quick-setting jelly mixes, milk shakes
E410	locust bean gum (carob gum)	salad cream
E412	guar gum	packet soups, meringue mixes, sauces
E413	tragacanth	salad dressings, processed cheese, cream cheese
E414	gum arabic (acacia)	confectionery
E415	xanthan gum	sweet pickle, coleslaw, horseradish cream
416	karaya gum	soft cheese, brown sauce
430	polyoxyethylene (8) stearate	
431	polyoxyethylene (40) stearate	
432	polyoxyethylene (20) sorbitan monolaurate (Polysorbate 20)	
433	polyoxyethylene (20) sorbitan mono-oleate (Polysorbate 80)	bakery products, confectionery creams, cakes
434	polyoxyethylene (20) sorbitan monopalmitate (Polysorbate 40)	
435	polyoxyethylene (20) sorbitan monostearate (Polysorbate 60)	
436	polyoxyethylene (20) sorbitan tristearate (Polysorbate 65)	
E440(a)	pectin	
E440(b)	amidated pectin	jams, preserves, desserts
	pectin extract	
442	ammonium phosphatides	cocoa and chocolate products

E460	microcrystalline cellulose; alpha-cellulose (powdered cellulose)	
E461	methylcellulose	high-fibre bread, grated cheese, low-fat spreads, edible ices, gâteaux
E463	hydroxypropylcellulose	
E464	hydroxypropylmethylcellulose	
E465	ethylmethylcellulose	
E466	carboxymethylcellulose, sodium salt (CMC)	jelly, pie filling
E470	sodium, potassium and calcium salts of fatty acids	cake mixes
E471	mono- and di-glycerides of fatty acids	
E472(a)	acetic acid esters of mono- and di-glycerides of fatty acids	
E472(b)	lactic acid esters of mono- and di-glycerides of fatty acids	frozen desserts, dessert toppings, mousse mixes, continental sausages, bread, frozen pizza
E472(c)	citric acid esters of mono- and di-glycerides of fatty acids	
E472(e)	mono- and diacetyltartaric acid esters of mono- and di-glycerides of fatty acids	
E473	sucrose esters of fatty acids	coatings for fruit
E474	sucroglycerides	edible ices
E475	polyglycerol esters of fatty acids	cakes and gâteaux
476	polyglycerol esters of polycondensed fatty acids of castor oil (polyglycerol polyricinoleate)	chocolate-flavour coatings for cakes
E477	propane-1, 2-diol esters of fatty acids	instant desserts
478	lactylated fatty acid esters of glycerol and propane-1, 2-diol	
E481	sodium stearoyl-2-lactylate	bread, cakes, biscuits, gravy granules
E482	calcium stearoyl-2-lactylate	
E483	stearyl tartrate	
491	sorbitan monostearate	
492	sorbitan tristearate	
493	sorbitan monolaurate	cake mixes
494	sorbitan mono-oleate	
495	sorbitan monopulmitate	
	dioctyl sodium sulphosuccinate	used in sugar refining to help crystallisation
	extract of quillaia	used in soft drinks to promote foam
	oxidatively polymerised soya bean oil	emulsions used to grease bakery tins
	polyglycerol esters of dimerised fatty acids of soya bean oil	

Sweeteners

Number	Name	Products in which found
	acesulfame potassium	canned foods, soft drinks, table-top sweeteners
	Aspartame	soft drinks, yoghurts, dessert and drink mixes, sweetening tablets
	hydrogenated glucose syrup	
	isomalt	
E421	mannitol	sugar-free confectionery
	saccharin	
	sodium saccharin	soft drinks, cider, sweetening tablets
	calcium saccharin	
E420	sorbitol; sorbitol syrup	sugar-free confectionery, jams for diabetics
	thaumatin	table-top sweeteners, yoghurt
	xylitol	sugar-free chewing gum

Others

Number	Name	Products	Use
E170	calcium carbonate		base, firming or release agent
E260	acetic acid	} pickles, crisps, salad cream, bread	} acid/acidity regulators
E261	potassium acetate		
E262	sodium hydrogen diacetate		
262	sodium acetate		
E263	calcium acetate	quick-set jelly mix	firming agent
E270	lactic acid	salad dressing, margarine	acid, antifungal action
E290	carbon dioxide	fizzy drinks	carbonating agent, packaging gas
296	DL-malic acid; L-malic acid	low-calorie squash, soup	acid
297	fumaric acid	soft drinks, sweets, biscuits, dessert mixes, pie fillings	acid
E325	sodium lactate	jams, preserves, sweets, flour confectionery	buffer/humectant
E326	potassium lactate }	jams, preserves, jellies, canned fruit, fruit pie filling }	} buffer/humectant
E327	calcium lactate		
E330	citric acid	many products	acid
E331	sodium dihydrogen citrate (monosodium citrate); disodium citrate; trisodium citrate	} sweets, gâteaux mixes, soft drinks, jams, preserves, sweets, processed cheese, canned fruit, dessert mixes	} acid/flavour buffer, sequestrants, calcium salts are firming agents
E332	potassium dihydrogen citrate (monopotassium citrate); tripotassium citrate		
E333	monocalcium citrate; dicalcium citrate; tricalcium citrate		
E334	L-(+)-tartaric acid	} confectionery, drinks, preserves, meringue pie mix, soft drinks, biscuit creams and fillings, dessert mixes, processed cheese	} acid/flavouring, buffer, emulsifying salts, sequestrants
E335	monosodium L-(+)-tartrate; disodium L-(+)-tartrate		
E336	monopotassium L-(+)-tartrate (cream of tartare); dipotassium L-(+)-tartrate		
E337	potassium sodium L-(+)-tartrate		
E338	orthophosphoric acid (phosphoric acid)	} soft drinks, cocoa, dessert mixes, non-dairy creamers, processed cheese	} acid/flavouring, sequestrants, emulsifying agents, buffers
E339	sodium dihydrogen orthophosphate; disodium hydrogen orthophosphate; trisodium orthophosphate		
E340	potassium dihydrogen orthophosphate; dipotassium hydrogen orthophosphate; tripotassium orthophosphate		
E341	calcium tetrahydrogen diorthophosphate; calcium hydrogen orthophosphate; tricalcium diorthophosphate		
350	sodium malate, sodium hydrogen malate }	} jams, sweets, cakes, biscuits, processed fruit and vegetables	} buffers, humectants, calcium salts are firming agents in canned fruit and vegetables
351	potassium malate		
352	calcium malate, calcium hydrogen malate		
353	metatartaric acid	wine	sequestrant

Number	Name	Use in	Function
355	adipic acid	sweets, synthetic cream desserts	buffer/flavouring
363	succinic acid	dry food and beverage mixes	buffer/flavouring
370	1,4-heptonolactone	dried soups, instant desserts	acid, sequestrant
375	nicotinic acid	bread, flour, breakfast cereals	colour stabiliser, nutrient
380	triammonium citrate	processed cheese	buffer, emulsifying salt
381	ammonium ferric citrate	bread	iron supplement
385	calcium disodium ethylenediamine-NNN'N'-tetra-acetate (calcium disodium EDTA)	canned shellfish	sequestrant
E422	glycerol	cake icing, confectionery	humectant, solvent
E450(a)	disodium dihydrogen diphosphate, trisodium diphosphate, tetrasodium diphosphate, tetra-potassium diphosphate	whipping cream, meat products, bread, processed cheese, canned vegetables	buffers, sequestrants, emulsifying salts, stabilisers, raising agents
E450(b)	pentasodium triphosphate, pentapotassium triphosphate		
E450(c)	sodium polyphosphates, potassium polyphosphates		
500	sodium carbonate, sodium hydrogen carbonate (bicarbonate of soda), sodium sesquicarbonate	jams, jellies, self-raising flour, wine, cocoa, biscuits, icing sugar	bases, aerating agents, anti-caking agents
501	potassium carbonate, potassium hydrogen carbonate		
503	ammonium carbonate; ammonium hydrogen carbonate		
504	magnesium carbonate		
507	hydrochloric acid	tomato juice	processing aid
508	potassium chloride	table salt replacement	gelling agent, salt substitute
509	calcium chloride	canned fruit/vegetables	firming agent
510	ammonium chloride	bread	yeast food
513	sulphuric acid		
514	sodium sulphate	colours	diluent
515	potassium sulphate	salt	salt substitute
516	calcium sulphate	bread	firming agent, yeast food
518	magnesium sulphate	bread	firming agent
524	sodium hydroxide	cocoa, jams, sweets	base
525	potassium hydroxide	sweets	base
526	calcium hydroxide	sweets	firming agent, neutralising agent
527	ammonium hydroxide	cocoa, food colouring	diluent and solvent for food colours, base
528	magnesium hydroxide	sweets	base
529	calcium oxide	sweets	base
530	magnesium oxide	cocoa products	anti-caking agent
535	sodium ferrocyanide	salt, wine	anti-caking agent
536	potassium ferrocyanide		
540	dicalcium diphosphate	cheese	buffer, neutralising agent
541	sodium aluminium phosphate	cake mixes, self-raising flour, biscuits	acid, raising agent
542	edible bone phosphate		anti-caking agent
544	calcium polyphosphates	processed cheese	emulsifying salt
545	ammonium polyphosphates	frozen chicken	emulsifier, texturiser
551	silicon dioxide (silica)	skimmed milk powder, sweeteners	anti-caking agent

552	calcium silicate	icing sugar, sweets	anti-caking agent, release agent
553(a)	magnesium silicate synthetic; magnesium trisilicate	sugar confectionery	anti-caking agent
553(b)	talc	tabletted confectionery	release agent
554	aluminium sodium silicate	packet noodles	anti-caking agent
556	aluminium calcium silicate		anti-caking agent
558	bentonite		anti-caking agent
559	kaolin		anti-caking agent
570	stearic acid		anti-caking agent
572	magnesium stearate	confectionery	emulsifier, release agent
575	D-glucono-1,5-lactone (glucono delta-lactone)	cake mixes, continental sausages	acid, sequestrant
576	sodium gluconate	dietary supplement, jams, dessert mixes	sequestrants, buffer, firming agent
577	potassium gluconate		
578	calcium gluconate		
620	L-glutamic acid	savoury foods and snacks, soups, sauces, meat products	flavour enhancers
621	sodium hydrogen L-glutamate (monosodium glutamate; MSG)		
622	potassium hydrogen L-glutamate (monopotassium glutamate)		
623	calcium dihydrogen di-L-glutamate (calcium glutamate)		
627	guanosine 5'-disodium phosphate (sodium guanylate)		
631	inosine 5'-disodium phosphate (sodium inosinate)		
635	sodium 5'-ribonucleotide		
636	maltol	cakes and biscuits	flavourings and flavour enhancers
637	ethyl maltol		
900	dimethylpolysiloxane		anti-foaming agent
901	beeswax	sugar, chocolate confectionery	glazing agent
903	carnauba wax	sugar, chocolate confectionery	glazing agent
904	shellac	apples	waxing agent
905	mineral hydrocarbons	dried fruit	glazing/coating agent
907	refined microcrystalline wax	chewing gum	release agent
920	L-cysteine hydrochloride	bread, cake, biscuit dough	flour treatment agents to improve texture
924	potassium bromate		
925	chlorine		
926	chlorine dioxide		
927	azodicarbonamide		
	aluminium potassium sulphate	chocolate-coated cherries	firming agent
	2-aminoethanol	caustic lye used to peel vegetables	base
	ammonium dihydrogen orthophosphate, diammonium hydrogen othophosphate	yeast food	buffer
	ammonium sulphate	yeast food	
	benzoyl peroxide	flour	bleaching agent
	butyl stearate		release agent
	calcium heptonate	prepared fruit and vegetables	firming agent, sequestrant
	calcium phytate	wine	sequestrant

dichlorodifluoromethane	frozen food	propellant and liquid freezant
diethyl ether		solvent
disodium dihydrogen ethylenediamine-NNN'N'-tetra-acetate (disodium dihydrogen EDTA)	brandy	sequestrant
ethanol (ethyl alcohol)		
ethyl acetate		
glycerol mono-acetate (monoacetin)	food colours, flavourings	solvent, dilutent
glycerol di-acetate (diacetin)		
glycerol tri-acetate (triacetin)		
glycine		sequestrant, buffer, nutrient
hydrogen		packaging gas
nitrogen		packaging gas
nitrous oxide	whipped cream	propellant in aerosol packs
octadecylammonium acetate	yeast foods in bread	anti-caking agent
oxygen		packaging gas
oxystearin	salad cream	sequestrant, fat crystallization inhibitor
polydextrose	reduced and low calorie foods	bulking agent
propan-1,2-diol (propylene glycol)	colourings and flavourings	solvent
propan-2-ol (isopropyl alcohol)		
sodium helptonate	edible oils	sequestrant
spermaceti		release agent
sperm oil		release agent

Crossword answers

Crossword A

Across   1 conduction; 4 fibre; 7 rice; 8 amino; 9 milk; 10 age; 11 onion; 14 sugary; 16 solubility; 18 soya protein; 20 oysters; 21 rag; 22 tea; 24 eat; 26 salty; 28 value; 29 hens; 32 biological; 33 stir; 34 tin; 35 iron; 36 bacteria

Down   1 cereals; 2 NACNE; 3 carbohydrate; 4 flour; 5 radiation; 6 bakery; 8 acids; 12 quantity; 13 microwave; 15 glycogen; 17 ovens; 18 starch; 19 joule; 23 plaster; 25 aspic; 27 lipid; 30 calor; 31 UHT

Crossword B

Across   1 salmonella; 5 moulds; 6 desert; 8 increase; 10 old; 11 ring; 12 oasis; 13 hat; 14 lid on; 17 stove; 18 taste; 21 lecithin; 22 chalaza; 24 indigestible; 27 cocci; 29 emulsion; 30 agar agar; 32 store in a fridge

Down   1 sodium; 2 listeria; 3 nutrients; 4 acidity; 5 microbe; 7 yoghurt; 9 essential; 15 emulsifier; 16 stock ledger; 19 acid; 20 bins; 23 zinc; 25 gums; 26 tannin; 27 cured; 28 suet; 31 roe

Crossword A

Across

1 The way heat travels in a solid (10)
4 Not a nutrient but essential to our diet (5)
7 Accompaniment to curry (4)
8 & 8 down Building blocks of proteins (5, 5)
9 Used to make cheese (4)
10 To be taken into consideration when planning menus (3)
11 A vegetable to make your eyes water (5)
14 Lactosey, maltosey, glucosey, _____ (6)
16 Property of vitamins A & D in fats; vitamins C & B in water (10)
18 Alternative to meat (4, 7)
20 A potential source of food-poisoning found in a bed (7)
21 Used by a chef – may cross-contaminate (3)
22 Afternoon _____ (3)
24 What we do with food (3)
26 Food that's too _____ is bad for blood pressure (5)
28 See 32 across
29 Source of *Salmonella* (4)
32 & 28 Indicates the number of essential amino acids in a protein (10, 5)
33 You must do this to a sauce to prevent it burning (4)
34 Can cause chemical food-poisoning (3)
35 Lack of it causes anaemia (4)
36 Cause of food-poisoning (8)

Down

1 Wheat, barley, oats are _____ (7)
2 'Less sugar, less fat, more fibre.' Which report? (5)
3 It gives us energy (12)
4 A form of starch (5)
5 Heat transfer in a grill (9)
6 Where bread is cooked and sold (6)
8 See 8 across
12 Vitamin C is found in large _____ in lemons (8)
13 & 17 Magnetrons and paddles are found in these (9, 5)
15 Polysaccharide storage in animals (8)
17 See 13 down
18 Doesn't dissolve but gelatinises (6)
19 The unit of energy (5)
23 Should be coloured and waterproof (7)
25 Jelly? (5)
27 A fat or oil is a _____ (5)
30 Type of gas (5)
31 Kills bacteria in milk (3)

Crossword B

Across

1 Bacteria found in eggs (10)
5 They give the blue vein to blue cheeses (6)
6 A place where camels live. Sounds like a pudding (6)
8 Incidents of food-poisoning are on the _____ (8)
10 A broiler is an _____ chicken (3)
11 Should be removed before handling food (4)
12 Water and trees in a desert (5)
13 Sits on a chef's head (3)
14 The way to cook vegetables (3, 2)
17 Used to cook on (5)
18 Important aspect of food preparation (5)
21 Emulsifier found in egg yolks (8)
22 Keeps the yolk in the middle of the egg (7)
24 Fibre is _____ (12)
27 Round-shaped bacteria (5)
29 Mixture of oil and water (8)
30 An alternative to gelatine for vegetarians (4, 4)
32 Do this with raw fish, meat and dairy products (5, 2, 1, 6)

Down

1 Essential mineral (6)
2 Bacteria in cook-chill foods (8)
3 Carbohydrates, proteins, fats, vitamins and minerals (9)
4 Low pH value acts as a preservative (7)
5 A fungus or bacterium is a _____ (7)
7 Bacterially preserved milk (7)
9 Some amino acids are _____ (9)
15 Glycerol monostearate is an artificial _____ (10)
16 Essential to stock rotation (5, 6)
19 Conditions found in the stomach (4)
20 Used to store waste (4)
23 A heavy metal (4)
25 Hold teeth (4)
26 Found in tea and red wine (6)
27 Bacon and ham are _____ (5)
28 Saturated fat found in animals (4)
31 Basis for taramasalata (3)

THE INSTITUTION OF ENVIRONMENTAL HEALTH OFFICERS
Chadwick House   Rushworth Street   London SE1 0QT
INTERMEDIATE EXAMINATION
May 1987

IMPORTANT: You are allowed two hours for answering this paper.

PART 1
Answer *ALL TWENTY* questions.

1 Name three high risk foods.
2 What food is most commonly implicated in outbreaks of Salmonella Food Poisoning?
3 State three benefits of Food Hygiene Education.
4 What is a bacterial spore?
5 State two ways in which bacteria can be killed.
6 Why should a cut finger be covered with a waterproof plaster?
7 List three causes of food spoilage.
8 Why is it important to cool food before it is to be stored in a refrigerator?
9 Name three methods of preserving food using high temperatures.
10 State three characteristics required for a floor in a kitchen.
11 Why should the junction of a kitchen wall and floor be coved or curved?
12 State three disadvantages of using open windows to ventilate a food preparation room.
13 What is a Sanitiser?
14 State two benefits of satisfactory cleaning.
15 List three visible signs of a rodent infestation.
16 Which two insects are the main pests in food areas?
17 Why is smoking illegal in food rooms?
18 Why should a refrigerator not be overloaded?
19 State three of the most common "foreign bodies" found in food.
20 Define food poisoning briefly in your own words.

Glossary

aerobic   term used to indicate the presence of oxygen, e.g. aerobic bacteria are bacteria that need oxygen in order to survive.

alimentary canal   the structure where digestion, absorption and egestion of food take place, beginning with the mouth and ending at the anus.

amino acids   the building blocks of proteins. Individual amino acids are joined in chains and held together by chemical bonds to form protein structures.

amylase   enzymes that break down starch to produce maltose. Found mainly in saliva in the mouth.

anaerobic   term used to indicate the absence of oxygen, e.g. anaerobic bacteria can live without oxygen.

anti-caking agents   substances added to dried foods to prevent them absorbing moisture, e.g. magnesium oxide added to table salt allows it to flow freely because the additive absorbs any moisture that would cause the salt to clump.

antioxidants   chemicals, including naturally occurring substances like vitamin C and vitamin E, which when added to foods prevent them absorbing oxygen and developing 'off flavours'; especially good for preventing rancidity in fats.

anus   the final part of the alimentary canal, through which the faeces are egested from the body.

ascorbic acid   vitamin C; can be used as an antioxidant.

Aspartame   a sweetener nearly 200 times as sweet as sucrose. Does not have an aftertaste; is used as an artificial sweetener.

binary fission   the process by which bacteria divide and reproduce, i.e. a single bacterium divides into two.

biological value   a percentage indicating the number of essential amino acids a food supplies to the body, e.g. a food having a biological value of 100% (eggs) contains all the essential amino acids, whereas a food with a lower biological value is missing some of the essential amino acids.

blanching   immersing food briefly in boiling water, usually prior to freezing, canning or drying, to destroy external enzymes.

botulism   a form of food-poisoning, usually fatal, caused by the bacterium *Clostridium botulinum.*

cellulose   a polysaccharide which makes up the wall of plant cells. As humans lack the necessary enzymes to break down cellulose, it passes through the alimentary canal undigested, and forms the roughage part of our diet.

chemical digestion   the breakdown of food into its smaller parts, i.e. nutrients, by enzymes.

chyme   the name given to food when it leaves the stomach.

combination method   method of cooking in which heat is transferred to the food by a dry method, e.g. frying, then by a moist method, e.g. stewing.

conduction   passage of heat or an electric current from one place to another through a solid object, i.e. a conductor like metal.

convection   movement of heat from one place to another through liquids or gases.

digestion   the process whereby large food particles are broken down into the nutrients they contain, which can then be absorbed into the bloodstream and taken to all parts of the body.

disaccharides   the group name for sugars formed when two monosaccharides combine, e.g. sucrose (fructose + glucose) and maltose (glucose + glucose).

dry method   method of cooking where heat is transferred to the surface of food by convection or radiation, e.g. roasting, baking or grilling. High temperatures are used.

duodenum   the first part of the small intestine, where enzymes are released to break down food into its nutrients.

emulsifier   an emulsifying agent, e.g. lecithin, found in egg yolks.

emulsifying agent   a substance, e.g. egg yolk (lecithin), that will stabilise an emulsion and prevent separation of the oil–water mixture, as in mayonnaise.

emulsion   mixture of oil and water, e.g. vinaigrette (vinegar and oil), which can only be mixed together by constant shaking. Such mixtures can be prevented from separating by adding emulsifying agents such as egg yolk.

enzymes   naturally occurring catalysts. They are responsible for the life processes of plants and animals and can affect foods, causing changes in texture, colour and flavour.

essential amino acids   amino acids the body cannot make, but must have, and which can only be obtained through the diet.

exponential phase   the growth phase of microbes that follows the lag phase. Here the cells are dividing at their maximum rate and reach very large numbers in relatively short periods of time.

fatty acid   component of fats and oils (lipids). May be saturated or mono/poly-unsaturated depending on their source. Animal fat contains mainly saturated fatty acids and plant oils mainly unsaturated fatty acids.

fibre   the indigestible parts of food, mainly from plant origin. Important for maintaining the correct functioning of the digestive system. NACNE recommends 30 g per day minimum.

flash point   the temperature at which a heated fat bursts into flames.

fructose   the sugar found in honey and fruits. It is very sweet, being about one and a half times as sweet as sucrose.

gastric juice   a 'cocktail' of enzymes, which bring about the breakdown of foodstuffs into the nutrients they contain.

gel   substance produced as a result of gelatinisation, e.g. a cornflour starch gel like blancmange.

gelatinisation   the process whereby polysaccharides, e.g. starch, absorb water and swell.

glucose   a monosaccharide about three-quarters as sweet as sucrose.

gluten   protein found in wheat flour, makes bread dough elastic.

glycerol   combines with fatty acids to form fats and oils. Common name is glycerine, which is a clear, thick, sweet liquid.

HTST (high-temperature short-holding pasteurisation)   pasteurisation of milk by heating to 72 °C for 15 seconds only.

humectants   substances added to products to keep them moist, e.g. glycerol. They have the opposite effect to anti-caking agents.

ileum   the second part of the small intestine, where digested nutrients are absorbed into the bloodstream.

incubation period   the time between ingestion of bacteria and the onset of disease symptoms, during which time the bacteria are multiplying.

infective dose   the number of bacteria needed to be consumed before symptoms of illness show.

infective food-poisoning   caused by the ingestion of food contaminated with large numbers (exceeding the infective dose) of live bacteria.

insulator   opposite of conductor. A medium that will not conduct heat or electricity, e.g. plastic, wood.

irradiation   the use of ionising radiation from radioactive sources, e.g. caesium 137, to kill microbes in food.

kilocalorie (kcal)   old unit of energy, but still used extensively. 1 kcal = 4.2 kJ.

kilojoule (kJ)   international unit of energy.

lactose   sugar found in milk. A disaccharide of galactose and glucose with a sweetness about one-sixth that of sucrose.

lag phase   the time taken for small numbers of bacteria to acclimatise to their surroundings before beginning rapid multiplication.

large intestine   the second part of the intestine, leading on from the small intestine. Here excess water is removed and the faeces are formed.

lecithin   an emulsifying agent.

lipid splitting   breaking up of lipids into fatty acids and glycerol, caused by excessive heating/re-heating. Reduces efficiency of the cooking lipid.

lipids   general term for fats and oils. Lipids are made up of two units, fatty acids and glycerol.

low fat   food from which virtually all fat has been removed, e.g. skimmed milk.

LTST (low-temperature long-holding pasteurisation)   pasteurisation of milk by heating to 63–65 °C and holding this temperature for 30 minutes.

macronutrients   those nutrients needed in large quantities daily, e.g. carbohydrates, fats and proteins.

maltose   a disaccharide sugar made up of two glucose units. It is found in barley grains and is released during the malting process in beer making. Has a sweetness one-third that of sucrose.

mechanical digestion   the breakdown of food into smaller manageable pieces by the teeth and stomach.

microbe   shortened version of the term micro-organism.

micronutrients   those nutrients needed in small or minute quantities daily, e.g. vitamins and minerals.

micro-organism   any living organism that can only be seen using a microscope, i.e. bacteria, viruses, certain fungi, algae and animals called protozoa.

moist method   method of cooking where heat is transferred to food by convection currents in a cooking liquid, e.g. poaching, boiling and stewing.

monosaccharides   group name for the simplest sugars, e.g. glucose and fructose.

mould   type of fungus causing decay of foodstuffs, especially fruits. Some are useful, e.g. *Penicillium roquefortii*, the blue mould of cheeses like Stilton.

nutrients   the chemical substances needed by living organisms in order to live, e.g. proteins, carbohydrates, lipids, vitamins, minerals.

nutrition   the study of the composition of food and how it is used by the body.

nutritive additives   vitamins and minerals added to foods to ensure a balanced diet, e.g. vitamins A and D are added to margarine, and calcium is added to white flour.

osmosis   process by which water moves across cell membranes and is taken up by micro-organisms. If microbes are placed in a highly concentrated solution, e.g. a high-salt solution, then instead of the bacteria taking up water, the water will be drawn out of the cells and the bacterium will shrivel and die.

oxidation   the chemical process where oxygen is added to foods resulting in 'off flavours', e.g. rancidity in fats. Can be prevented by antioxidants.

pasteurisation   heat process used to reduce the number of bacteria in a food and so prolong its shelf-life, e.g. pasteurised milk. The process does not appreciably alter the taste of the product.

pathogenic bacteria   bacteria capable of causing disease.

pectin   a polysaccharide that sticks plant cells together. Used to set jam.

photosynthesis   the process by which plants convert the sun's light energy into food, namely glucose and starch. From these simple molecules all the other nutrients can be made.

polysaccharides   long chains of monosaccharides, e.g. starch is a long chain of glucose units. They are not sweet and do not dissolve in water.

pyrethrum   a permitted insecticide for use in food rooms.

Quorn   trade name for a fungal protein used as a substitute for meat. It has a fibrous texture similar to meat, can absorb flavours and has the advantage of being low in fat.

radiation   the movement of heat away from a hot object.

rancidity   a chemical change in fats, leading to 'off' odours and tastes caused by oxidation.

rectum   the last region of the large intestine, where the faeces are stored before defaecation through the anus.

roughage   a term used to mean dietary fibre.

saccharin   an artificial sweetener with a sweetness 550 times that of sucrose.

saturated   term given to fats containing no double bonds in their fatty-acid structure. Mainly of animal origin; thought to be implicated in heart disease.

small intestine   the first part of the alimentary canal leading from the stomach. It is here that the chyme is digested by enzymes and the resulting nutrients absorbed into the bloodstream.

smoke point   the temperature reached when a heated fat starts to emit smoke.

spore   highly resistive structure produced by certain types of bacteria to enable them to survive adverse conditions such as high temperatures or periods of dehydration. They are very difficult to destroy and can only be killed by sterilisation.

stabilisers   substances able to absorb large quantities of water, so making them good thickening agents and emulsifiers, e.g. gelatine and gums.

sterilisation   the destruction of all microbial life, including spores. The process alters the taste of foods, as in sterilised milk.

sucrose   most commonly used sugar for consumption. Extracted from sugar cane and sugar beet, it is a disaccharide of fructose and glucose, and is given a sweetness value of one for comparison with other sugars.

toxic food-poisoning   caused by the ingestion of food contaminated with toxic chemicals, which may or may not have been produced by bacteria.

UHT (ultra heat treatment)   a form of HTST, where prolonged storage time is achieved by heating milk to 132 °C for at least one second.

unsaturated   term given to fats which contain one or more double bond in their fatty-acid structure. Mainly of vegetable origin.

yeast   a single-celled fungus, which reproduces by a process called budding. Yeasts convert sugar to alcohol and carbon dioxide in a process called fermentation, so are useful in making bread, beer and wine.

Index